FIVE STAR ENGLISH

FIVE STAR ENGLISH

for the hotel and tourist industry

Rod Revell   Chris Stott

Oxford University Press

Oxford University Press
Walton Street, Oxford OX2 6DP

Oxford New York Toronto
Delhi Bombay Calcutta Madras Karachi
Petaling Jaya Singapore Hong Kong Tokyo
Nairobi Dar es Salaam Cape Town
Melbourne Auckland

and associated companies in
Berlin Ibadan

OXFORD and OXFORD ENGLISH are trade
marks of Oxford University Press

ISBN 0 19 437641 9

Printed in Hong Kong

Contents

Acknowledgements

The authors and publisher would like to thank the following for their advice and assistance in the preparation of this course:

Air Transport and Travel Industry Training Board Library, Staines, Middlesex
Hotel and Catering Industry Training Board, Wembley, Middlesex
Hong Kong Tourist Association, London
Leeds Polytechnic, School of Hospitality Management and Home Economics
Spanish National Tourist Office
Thomson Holidays
Viking Hotel, York
West Yorkshire Language Link, Bradford
York City Council, Tourism Department
York College of Arts and Technology, Department of Community Studies
Yorkshire and Humberside Tourist Board

For permission to use adapted material for facsimiles:

ABC Airlines Guide p. 40
British Rail pp. 118; 140; 141
British Telecom p. 10
British Tourist Authority p. 112
City and Guilds of London Institute, exam paper 709 p. 57
Guardian (17.1.81), compiler Catherine Jones p. 56
Hong Kong Tourist Association, *Meeting Guide to Hong Kong* pp. 146-56
Letts Holiday Guides p. 73
Pegasus Holidays (London) Ltd. p. 159

For photographs:

J. Allan Cash p. 55
Chris Andrews p. 61
BBC p. 83
British Tourist Authority p. 133
Campaign for Real Ale (CAMRA) p. 132
Documentation Française p. 60
Hong Kong Government Office p. 145
Hong Kong Tourist Association p. 145
Hoskyns Hotel Systems p. 10
Terry Williams p. 72
Yorkshire and Humberside Tourist Board pp. 111; 123; 157

Illustrations by:

Wendy Brett
Peter Ferris
Jim Robbins
Barry Rowe

The following location photographs were taken by Paul Simms, Photographs and All That, Oxford: pp. 9; 10; 21; 33; 43; 94; 105.

Special thanks for help with these location photographs are due to the Royal Lancaster Hotel, London; Quincey's Restaurant, Oxford, and the Randolph Hotel, Oxford.

And, finally, the authors would like to acknowledge the encouragement and forbearance of colleagues at York Language Training Ltd. during the writing of this book.

Teacher's notes

---
1 Aims of the course

Five Star English is designed to improve the job-specific English of non-native speakers of the language who are working, or being trained for subsequent careers, in the tourist industry. These include staff with customer contact in hotels and restaurants, travel agents, tour operators, and employees of state and local tourist organizations. The functional aspects of the industry that are covered in the course range from the relatively limited language routines of, for example, receptionists and waiters to the more advanced language skills required by managers and those involved in setting up tour operations. The carefully controlled introduction of new language items in the course is matched by a parallel development in the professional content from the simple to the more complex. New language items are thus introduced and exemplified in terms of existing knowledge.

Five Star English aims to practise and develop the four skills of listening, speaking, reading, and writing through the use of varied and creative activities. Particular emphasis is placed on the first two of these skills.

Entry level

The course is intended for learners who are at a pre-intermediate level in English. It is designed to upgrade their ability to a tourism-specific intermediate stage on completion. Using the Council of Europe criteria as a reference, this implies a movement from a little below Waystage up to the Threshold level. The course is also suitable for learners at a somewhat higher entry level who either have not used their English for some years or wish to orientate a more general knowledge of the language towards one more appropriate to the needs of the tourist industry.

Methods of use

The course is designed both for use in a class setting, with a teacher, and for individual learners without access to a teacher.

Parts of the course

The course consists of this book and a cassette containing material for the listening and speaking activities in the course.

1

2 Structure of the course

The course consists of fifteen units. Twelve of these are main units with recorded material on the cassette. The other three are revision units (after Units 4, 8, and 12). Each of the main units deals with one particular aspect of the tourist industry. This topic is indicated by the title of the unit (see Contents List). The main units are all divided into six sections.

Reading and Listening

This section provides the main thematic and linguistic input for each unit. The reading passages are either informative texts or else based on or drawn from authentic written material used within the tourist industry such as Key Cards, guide books, and reports, and letters from and to tourist industry personnel. The listening passages comprise one or more dialogues between industry staff and their customers and colleagues, both face-to-face and on the phone. These are designed to encourage the extraction of both general and detailed information. The comprehension activities associated with this section frequently make use of ways of summarizing information that are customary in the tourist industry.

Language study

A number of language items that have been exemplified in the Reading and Listening section, and are felt to be appropriate to the professional topic of the unit and to the grading system that operates within the course, are taken out for detailed study and exercise. Both the approach to these items and the way they are exercised are varied.

Listening and Speaking

The emphasis on the oral/aural skills is underlined by the inclusion of a substantial listening and speaking section in each unit. The dialogues are longer in this section but introduce few unfamiliar language items. They provide consolidation of language work already done and give extensive listening practice. They also serve to familiarize the learner with a wide range of accents, mother tongue and foreign. As in the first section, the dialogues are accompanied by comprehension activities, usually based on the types of form used for recording information in tourist industry settings.

The speaking exercise is designed to give the learner active practice in the production of a key spoken pattern. The examples are printed in the coursebook but the rest of the exercise is solely on the cassette.

Activities

In each unit the Activities give the learner the opportunity to re-apply in new ways the job-specific language that has been learnt. The techniques most frequently used in this section are problem solving, information transfer and topic-based discussion.

Writing

Routine writing tasks of the type encountered in the tourist industry are practised in this section together with language devices, such as linking and sequencing, commonly used to structure information in written texts. Emphasis is placed on producing routine letters and telexes, expanding notes and, later in the course, on the production of intra-industry correspondence.

Word study

The final section in each unit is an alphabetically arranged list of the new words introduced in the unit. Each entry has a simple context-specific definition or, in a few cases, an illustration to make the meaning clear.

3 Classroom use

The course has been designed to provide approximately 70 hours of classroom work on the basis of five and a half hours per main unit and one and a half hours per revision unit. These timings should not, however, be taken as more than suggestions. The actual amount of work that is necessary will vary according to the level of the learners' English, their knowledge of the professional background, the amount of work that is done as homework, and adaptation by teachers to their own situation.

The notes on using the course in the classroom that follow are intended only as a guide. Teachers will find it necessary to adapt to the needs of their students.

Reading and Listening

Introduce the students to the theme of the text before they look at it. Check their general knowledge of the topic by asking questions relevant to their background. Ask the students to read the passage silently for its general meaning and then once again, looking up unfamiliar words in the Word Study if necessary, for a more precise understanding. Ask a few questions to make sure that the text is fairly well understood. Explain any difficulties there may be. Ask the students to write the answers to the comprehension questions. Go over the answers with the students. Write the correct answers on the board. Get the students to give you, orally, the main points of the passage.

Introduce the listening dialogues briefly. Play them through once without stopping so that the students can get a general idea of the contents. Discuss the dialogues with them and clear up any major misunderstandings. Play the dialogues again so that the students can do the comprehension exercise while they listen. Answers to this and to the other exercises in the unit should be written in notebooks and not in the coursebook. Discuss the students' answers with them. At this stage you may like to play the dialogue again and allow the students to read it at the same time in order to check their understanding. In any case, they should not have looked at the text of the dialogues before this stage.

Language study

Introduce each of the language points that are covered in the exercises in this section. Discuss any difficulties and refer back to the occurrences of the exponents in Reading and Listening to help clarification. Provide further examples if necessary. Ask the students to do the exercises, providing assistance where necessary. Check the answers orally.

Listening and Speaking

The procedure for the listening comprehension here is basically the same as that outlined under Reading and Listening. However, the dialogues are longer and do not introduce significant new language items. As such, they can be used more extensively than the earlier ones.

Introduce the language teaching point that is exercised in the Speaking. Provide further examples if necessary. Ask the class to listen to the prompts on the tape and produce appropriate responses before they hear the model response. This work can be done by the whole class, groups, pairs, or individuals. A language laboratory, if available, is a useful aid when doing this exercise.

Activities

Introduce each activity, adding extra information if necessary. Brief the students on what has to be done before allowing them to attempt the activity. Make sure that they understand any non-verbal devices that are used and that they know exactly what has to be done. Discuss the solutions that are arrived at with the class as a whole.

Writing

Allow the students to read the model text or examples. Discuss any difficulties and make sure the principal objects of the exercise are understood. Ask the students to write their answers in class or for homework. If the work is done in class, give individual assistance. Check the students' work. Write a model answer on the board if necessary.

Self-study guide

For students using the course without a teacher.

Who is the course for?

If you know some English already and want to learn the sort of English that is useful in the tourist industry, then this course is suitable for you. It has been written for people who are already working, or will in the future be working, in hotels, restaurants, travel agencies, tour companies, etc. The aim of the course is to teach people like this the sort of English they will need in their work.

What will I learn?

You will learn to **understand** tourists and people in the tourist industry when they speak to you. Many of the voices you will hear on the cassette are British and American, but you will also hear how people from other parts of the world speak English. You will learn to **speak** in a way that will help people and will help you in your work. You will learn to **read** and **write** the English that is necessary for work in the tourist industry.

How can I use this course?

The course consists of a coursebook and a cassette. There are twelve main units in the course and three revision units. Each revision unit comes after four main units (after Units 4, 8, and 12) and checks that you still know what you learnt in those units. It is best if you work through the course from Units 1 to 12. The instructions below tell you what to do in each unit.

It is not possible to say how much time you will need for each unit. This depends on your knowledge of English and on your learning style. Work at the speed that is best for you. **Regular** practice is important. It is much better if you study for a short time often than to study for a long time but not often.

There is a Word Study section at the end of each main unit. This explains words in simple English. There is also a Word List at the back of the book (pages 193–199). If you have a dictionary, that will be useful too.

The answers to the Speaking exercises are on the cassette. The answers to all the other exercises are in the Key (pages 165–192). You can use this to check on your progress.

Section	Instructions
Reading and Listening	1 Read the text to get the general idea. 2 Read the text again in more detail. Look in Word Study and/or your dictionary. 3 Write answers to the Reading Check. 4 Check your answers in the Key (pages 165–192). 1 ■ Listen once to get the general idea. **Do not read** the dialogues in your coursebook. 2 ■ Listen again in more detail. Look in Word Study or your dictionary, if necessary. **Do not read** the dialogues in your coursebook. 3 ■ Listen again until you can understand. Write answers to the Listening Check. Only if absolutely necessary look at the text of the dialogues in your coursebook. 4 Check your answers in the Key.
Language study	1 Look at the examples in each exercise carefully. There are also examples in the Reading and Listening. Look at these too. 2 Write your answers for each of the exercises. 3 Check your answers in the Key.
Listening and Speaking	1–4 ■ Follow the instructions under Listening above. 1 ■ Listen to the examples and read them in your coursebook. 2 ■ Listen to the cassette. Speak your answers in the pauses. Listen to the answers on the tape. Do the exercise until your answers are the same.
Activities	1 Read the instructions carefully. 2 Look at the text and any other information. Try to give the answers asked for in the instructions. 3 Check your answers in the Key. 4 If your answers are not correct, look at the Activity again. Try to see why your answers are different.
Writing	1 Look at the examples carefully. 2 Do the writing exercise. 3 Check your answer in the Key.

The symbol ■ indicates the use of the cassette.

Unit 1
Enquiries and reservations

Reading and Listening

Reading

Try to understand the meaning of any new words or expressions while you are reading the passage. After that, look for new words and expressions in the Word Study at the end of the unit.

As you know, a receptionist works in one of the 'front offices' by the front hall or lobby of a hotel. Usually, all members of staff who work in these offices have direct personal or telephone contact with the guests.

In a large hotel, the receptionist welcomes and registers the guests. What about in a small hotel? Here the work of the receptionist may also include the job of advance reservations clerk, enquiry clerk, and book-keeper.

Telex

Computer terminal

Telephone

Letter

Personal contact

Telegram

Making advance reservations

The advance reservations clerk deals with reservation enquiries, of course, and with the booking and allocation of accommodation. A hotel receives reservation requests in different ways. For example, telephone bookings are the most common in many hotels. This is because these bookings are quick and it is possible to get full information from the customer. Hotels often ask people who make reservations by telephone to confirm their bookings in writing.

In many countries, reservations by telegram are less important than telex reservations. Why is this? Because the telex is fast and the confirmation is made immediately.

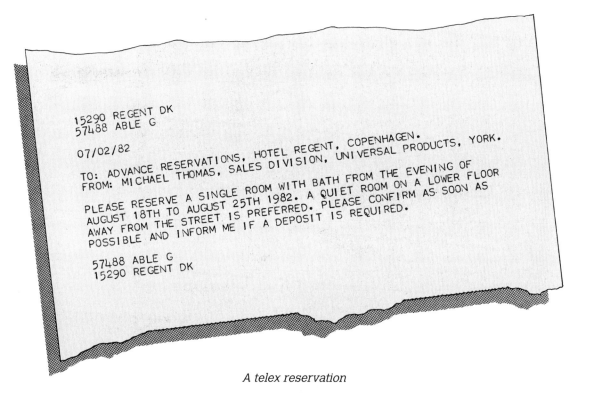

15290 REGENT DK
57488 ABLE G

07/02/82

TO: ADVANCE RESERVATIONS, HOTEL REGENT, COPENHAGEN.
FROM: MICHAEL THOMAS, SALES DIVISION, UNIVERSAL PRODUCTS, YORK.

PLEASE RESERVE A SINGLE ROOM WITH BATH FROM THE EVENING OF
AUGUST 18TH TO AUGUST 25TH 1982. A QUIET ROOM ON A LOWER FLOOR
AWAY FROM THE STREET IS PREFERRED. PLEASE CONFIRM AS SOON AS
POSSIBLE AND INFORM ME IF A DEPOSIT IS REQUIRED.

57488 ABLE G
15290 REGENT DK

A telex reservation

Perhaps you have seen that a number of hotels now have computer terminals. These hotels can link their reservation systems with other hotels in their group, with airline seat reservation systems and with terminals in the offices of important travel agents.

If a hotel is able to accept a booking, the reservations clerk must record it. The reservations clerk normally completes a reservation form and enters the information in a reservation diary.

Reading check

1 In what way is the work of a receptionist different in a large hotel and a small hotel?
2 Who does the allocation of hotel bedrooms?
3 Write down six ways that a hotel receives bookings. Which of these do you think is the least important?
4 When are guests asked to confirm a booking?
5 How does the reservations clerk record a booking?

Listening

Listen to the dialogue on the cassette before you read it in your book. Try to understand the meaning of any new words and expressions while you are listening to the dialogue. After that, look for new words and expressions in the Word Study at the end of the unit.

Mr Harvey is in the Accommodation Bureau at Copenhagen Central Railway Station. While you are listening to his conversation with Fru Nielsen, look at the hotel list below.

Name and address of hotel	Telephone Telex	No. of beds	Price (D.kr.) *= breakfast included					Full board per person
			min-max 🛏	🛁		min-max 🛏🛏	🚿	
			145	220	280	340		
Kastrup Hotel Kastruplundgade 28 DK-2770 Kastrup	01-172900 TLX. 31230	96						
Hotel Regent Jarmers Pläds 7 Dk-1551 Copenhagen V	01-689011 TLX.15290	184	180*	240–300*			360–400*	275– 375
Hotel Glostrup Hovedvejen 49 DK-2600 Glostrup	02-340028	168	160	240			320–350	
Hotel Titan Istedgade 17 DK-1650 Copenhagen V	01-112400 TLX.15919	212		270			350–400	300– 400
Union Hotel Vesterbrogade 239 DK-1620 Copenhagen V	01-244860 TLX.19284	204	180*	250–280*			350–410*	

Hotel list

Nielsen God morgen.
Harvey Excuse me, do you speak English?
Nielsen Yes, I do. How can I help you?
Harvey I need a double room with bath for two nights.
Nielsen I see. What sort of hotel would you like?
Harvey Well, could you tell me what kind of accommodation is available?

Nielsen Well, of course, there are different classes of hotel. Prices start at D.kr. 100 a night for a one star hotel and go up to D.kr. 650 for a better one.
Harvey What is there for about £30 a night?
Nielsen That's about 400 crowns. Here's a selection of hotels at around that price.
Harvey Ah, thank you very much.
Nielsen Where would you like to be?

The hotels in the centre are more convenient than the hotels in the suburbs, but then the city centre hotels are more expensive and noisier.

Harvey We'd like to be in the city centre. Which of these is a good place?

Nielsen Well, the Titan, the Union, and the Regent are all very central.

Harvey Could you explain the prices at the Regent?

Nielsen Yes. There is a minimum price for off-season stay and this maximum price for high season, June to August.

Harvey What's the Regent like?

Nielsen It's a medium-sized hotel and, as far as I know, it's very comfortable.

Harvey Can I book a room in the Regent from here?

Nielsen Certainly, that's no problem. So that's for today the 17th August, and tomorrow?

Harvey Yes.

Nielsen What name is it, please?

Harvey Harvey.

Nielsen Could you spell that?

Harvey H-A-R-V-E-Y.

Nielsen Thank you, Mr Harvey. Just wait a moment while I confirm your booking with the hotel.

Listening check

1 What kind of room does Mr Harvey want?
2 In what ways are suburban hotels better?
3 Must Mr Harvey pay the minimum or maximum price for a hotel room?
4 How big is the Hotel Regent?
5 For what dates does Mr Harvey need a room?

Language study

Requesting information

Notice how we can ask for information politely.

Examples:

You don't know the name and address of a customer. (tell)
▶ **Could** you tell me your name and address, please?

You don't know the spelling of a customer's name. (spell)
▶ **Would** you spell your name, please?

You aren't sure of the name of a company. (give)
▶ **Can** you give me the name of your company, please?

Using **could**, **would** and **can**, ask questions in a similar way.

1 You don't know the telephone number of a customer. (tell)
2 You aren't sure of the surname of a caller. (repeat)
3 You are unsure of the number of people in a group. (tell)
4 You don't know the arrival time of a customer. (give)
5 You don't know the spelling of a street name. (spell)
6 You are unsure of a guest's date of departure. (confirm)

Comparing

Study the following table.

	Station Hotel	Hotel Bristol	Hotel Park
1 How expensive is it? (D.kr.)	340	220	270
2 How quiet is it? (●)	●●	●	●●●
3 How convenient is it? (kms to centre)	2	1	4
4 How comfortable is it? (∗)	∗∗∗	∗	∗∗
5 How big is it? (number of beds)	400	680	250
6 How modern is it? (built in)	1947	1975	1964

Notice how we can make sentences comparing different hotels.

1 The Hotel Park is **more expensive than** the Bristol, but **less expensive than** the Station Hotel.
The Station Hotel is **the most expensive** and the Bristol is **the least expensive**.

2 The Station Hotel is **noisier than** the Park, but **quieter than** the Bristol.
The Bristol is **the noisiest** and the Park is **the quietest**.

Now write similar sentences about 3, 4, 5, and 6.

Numbers and dates

Notice how we say the following numbers and dates.

703 *seven hundred and three.*
521 *five hundred and twenty-one.*
3,845 *three thousand eight hundred and forty-five.*
Tel: 0904-37769 *oh nine oh four, three double seven six nine.*
Room 104 *room one hundred and four* **or** *room one oh four.*
30 January 1981∗ *the thirtieth of January, nineteen eighty-one.*

∗ We can also write 30th January or January 30th. In the USA it is:
January 30, 1981 *January thirtieth, nineteen eighty-one.*

Now say the following aloud.

2,714, 30th April 1983, tel: 08-58 23 62, 12,449, June 12, Room 317,
tel: 01-703 4468, 19 July, Room 502, 650, 5th floor, May 14 1982,
01-455 4011, 30 November 1982, 12th floor, 9th July 1984,
17,446.

Listening and Speaking

Mr Knudsen, the Advance Reservations Clerk at the Hotel Regent, is busy on the telephone. While you are listening to his telephone calls, complete Standard Reservation Forms like the one below. Remember, don't read the dialogues in your book or look in the Word Study until you have listened to them on the cassette.

Reservation form

Name of guest: Mr/Mrs/Miss/Ms ...... *James* ......

Address ...... *42 Station Road* ......

...... *York* ......

...... *YO2 1JG* ......

Telephone ...... *453 666* ......

Arrival date ......

am/pm ......

How many nights ......

Single ☐ Single bath ☐ Single shower ☐

Double ☐ Double bath ☐ Double shower ☐ Twin bath ☐

Clerk ......

Rate per night ......

How many people ......

Date ......

Standard reservation form

book a room
– in the Regent
– for next week

First caller

Operator Hotel Regent. Good morning. Can I help you?

Caller Yes, I'd like to book a room for next week.

Operator Hold the line, please, and I'll put you through to Advance Reservations.

Knudsen Advance Reservations. Can I help you?

Caller Yes, I'd like to book a twin-bedded room from the afternoon of the 21st August to the morning of the 27th.

Knudsen Yes, we have a twin-bedded room available for those dates. The rate is 390 crowns per night, including continental breakfast.

Caller That will be fine.

Knudsen Could I have your name and address, please?

Caller Yes, it's Mr James.

Knudsen J-A-M-E-S?

Caller Yes, that's right. 42, Station Road, York, England.

Knudsen Have you the post code, please?

Caller Yes. It's YO2 1JG.

Knudsen 42, Station Road, York YO2 1JG, England ... Good. And your telephone number?

Caller 0904-53666.

Knudsen Right. Thank you. I'll send you a reservation card by post confirming your booking, Mr James. And we look forward to your visit.

Caller Thank you very much. Goodbye.

Knudsen Goodbye, sir.

Second caller

Knudsen Advance Reservations. Can I help you?

Caller My name is Dalbret. I'd like to book a single room for 25th August.

Knudsen I'm very sorry, sir. We have no single rooms available on that date. I can put you on the waiting list and ring you if there's a cancellation.

Caller Thank you, but could you give me the name of another hotel?

Knudsen Try the Hotel Central, sir.

Caller Hotel Central. Thank you very much.

Knudsen Not at all. Thank you for calling.

Third caller

Caller Good morning. This is Frau Schmidt of Holstein AG, Hamburg. I want to reserve a single room for Herr Lang, our Marketing Manager.

Knudsen Yes, Frau Schmidt. When does he require the room?

Caller For the night of 24th August. And Herr Lang would like a quiet room away from the street.

Knudsen For 24th August. Certainly. Could you give me your address, please?

Caller Yes, it's Postweg 45, 2000 Hamburg 22.

Knudsen Could you spell 'Postweg', please?

Caller Yes, it's P-O-S-T-W-E-G.

Knudsen Postweg 45, 2000 Hamburg 22.

Caller Right. Oh, and would you send us the bill, please?

Knudsen Of course. And thank you for calling.

Caller Thank you. Goodbye.

Fourth caller

Knudsen Advance Reservations. Can I help you?

Caller Yes, do you have a double room with shower from the 19th to the 23rd August, with full board, please?

Knudsen One moment, please ... Yes, we have.

Caller What is the daily rate?

Knudsen D.Kr. 340 per person.

Caller Fine. Could I make a booking, please?

Knudsen Certainly. Your name, address and telephone number, please.

Caller My name is Roberts and the address is P.O. Box 743, NL-1017 Amsterdam. The telephone is 02-16 45 72. Could I also have garage space for my car?

Knudsen Certainly, Mr Roberts. I'll reserve you a space. Anything else, sir?

Caller No, that's all, thank you.

Knudsen I'll send you confirmation of your booking.

Caller Thank you very much. Goodbye.

Knudsen Goodbye.

Speaking
Requesting information

Study the following examples.

Head receptionist Find out Mrs Smith's full name and address.
Receptionist *Mrs Smith, could you tell me your full name and address, please?*

Head receptionist Find out the number in Mr Bourne's group.
Receptionist *Mr Bourne, could you tell me the number in your group, please?*

Now do the exercise on the tape, forming questions in a similar way. After you speak you will hear the receptionist's words on the tape.

Activities

The Hotel Regent has received bookings for the fortnight 17th–30th August by telex, from the local Accommodation Bureau and via the telephone. Go back to the listening passages to find this information. Now enter all these bookings using the Standard Reservation Chart below for the first floor of the hotel.

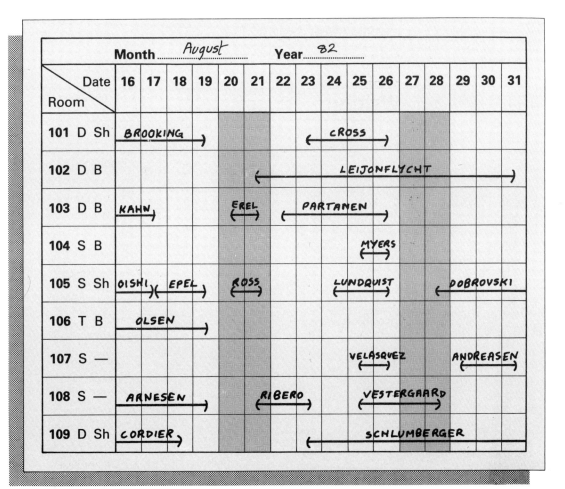

Room / Date	16	17	18	19	20	21	22	23	24	25	26	27	28	29	30	31
Month August **Year** 82																
101 D Sh	BROOKING →							← CROSS →								
102 D B							←	LEIJONFLYCHT								→
103 D B	KAHN →				← EREL →		← PARTANEN →									
104 S B										← MYERS →						
105 S Sh	OISHI →← EPEL →			← ROSS →			← LUNDQUIST →				← DOBROVSKI					
106 T B	OLSEN →															
107 S —										← VELASQUEZ →		← ANDREASEN →				
108 S —	ARNESEN →				← RIBERO →			← VESTERGAARD →								
109 D Sh	CORDIER →						←	SCHLUMBERGER								

Now answer these questions using the Standard Reservation Chart.

1 How many single rooms are available on the 23rd August?

2 A family would like to stay the night of Saturday 27th August. They want two double or twin-bedded rooms, or one of each, both with bath. Can you accept their booking?

3 How many people are staying on this floor on the 29th August?

4 A group of seven would like to stay on the 20th for one night. Is that possible?

5 Which night does this floor have the fewest guests?

In a small hotel, a receptionist does a number of jobs in order to satisfy the hotel's needs and the customer's needs. For example, the receptionist will:

prepare arrival/departure lists   *deal with correspondence*
welcome guests   *allocate rooms*
show guests to rooms   *take advance bookings*
deal with departures   *deal with guests' problems*
deal with cancellations, etc.   *deal with enquiries*

Place these jobs in what you think is their order of importance. Give reasons for your choice of order.

Writing

The Hotel International has received this letter.

```
                                              17 Lime Avenue,
                                              York,
                                              YO2 1PB
                                              England


                                          29th January 1982

The Manager,
Hotel International,
Amager Boulevard 162,
DK-2300 Copenhagen 5,
Denmark


Dear Sir,

My family and I stayed at your hotel when we visited Copenhagen last
year. We are now planning a second visit during May this year and
hope it will be possible to stay at the International again. We
require two twin-bedded rooms with baths for six nights from 7th May.
We would like rooms with a view over the park again, if possible.
Please let me know if a deposit is required.

Yours faithfully,


Peter Johnson


Peter Johnson
```

Here is the reply from the Hotel International.

HOTEL INTERNATIONAL

Amager Boulevard 162 · DK-2300 · Copenhagen 5 · Denmark   Telephone 01-107092 · Telex 15312

Mr Peter Johnson
17 Lime Avenue
York
YO2 1PB   7 February 1982
England

Dear Mr Johnson,

Thank you for your letter of 29 January 1982.

We have much pleasure in confirming your booking of two twin-bedded rooms with baths from 7th May – 12th May 1982, inclusive. Your rooms have a view over the park.

A deposit is not required.

We look forward to your visit.

Yours sincerely,

A Madsen

(Mr A. Madsen – Advance Reservations)

Using Mr Madsen's letter as an example, write letters of reply to the following reservation requests. You can accept all of these bookings.

1 Frank Giles, 45 Waterloo Road, Campellton, New Brunswick, Canada   Double Room/Shower   from 3.4.82   3 nights   Lower floor requested

2 Jose Gilbert, Perez Galdos 34, Valencia 8, Spain   Twin/Bath   from 2.6.82   7 nights   Quiet room requested

3 Sonia Gregory, 11 Lindman Road, Poole BH13 6BN, Dorset, England   Single   from 6.6.82   4 nights   Garage parking wanted

Word study

advance reservations p. 9, reservations made by guests before they arrive.

allocation of accommodation p. 11, deciding in which room each guest will stay.

available p. 12, ready for use.

Check (USA) **bill** p. 16, record of what the customer must pay. *v* **bill**.

booking p. 11, reservation. *v* **book**.

book-keeper p. 9, person who records money paid and received.

cancellation p. 16, message from a person with a booking saying he isn't coming. *v* **cancel**.

clerk p. 9, office worker.

common p. 11, usual.

computer terminals p. 11, electronic senders and receivers of information to and from a computer.

confirm p. 11, agree to a booking. *n* **confirmation**.

contact p. 9, communication.

continental breakfast p. 15, light breakfast.

convenient p. 13, in a useful position.

correspondence p. 18, letters.

customer p. 11, person using a hotel.

deals with p. 11, works with; handles.

deposit p. 11, money required to confirm a booking.

diary p. 11, daily record.

fortnight p. 17, two weeks.

full board p. 16, accommodation and all meals.

guests p. 9, people staying at a hotel.

high season p. 13, the part of the year with the most guests.

hold the line p. 15, wait.

link p. 11, connect.

medium-sized p. 13, between large and small.

members of staff p. 9, people who work in a hotel.

normally p. 11, usually.

off-season p. 13, the part of the year with the fewest guests.

put you through p. 15, connect you with.

rate p. 15, charge.

registers p. 9, records information about guests.

selection p. 12, choice. *v* **select**.

sort p. 12, type; kind.

suburbs p. 13, parts of a town outside the centre.

systems p. 11, ways of doing things.

travel agents p. 11, companies or people who sell journeys and holidays.

Can I speak with Mr Jones?
I put you through.

Unit 2
Reception

Reading and Listening

Reading

Try to understand the meaning of any new word or expression while you are reading the passage. After that, look for new words and expressions in the Word Study at the end of the unit.

It is important that the hotel receptionist should make sure that guests are registered correctly. A hotel register or, more usually, a registration card is used to record the full name, nationality, home address, and signature of each guest. Foreign visitors must provide additional information such as passport number and its place of issue, and their next destination. Many hotels use the registration card to find out more about their customers and ask questions about occupation, method of payment, and purpose of visit.

The receptionist should always check that the registration cards are completed correctly and legibly. What if there is a query? Well, then the receptionist should politely ask the guest for clarification. It is also necessary to make sure that the reservation details have not changed. After this the receptionist can inform the guest of the room number and rate.

What happens if the guest has a travel agency booking? With that sort of guest, the receptionist should obtain the original hotel voucher and check it against the hotel's copy. When large tour groups are checking in, it is useful for the tour leader to deal with the registration cards and hand them over to the reception desk himself.

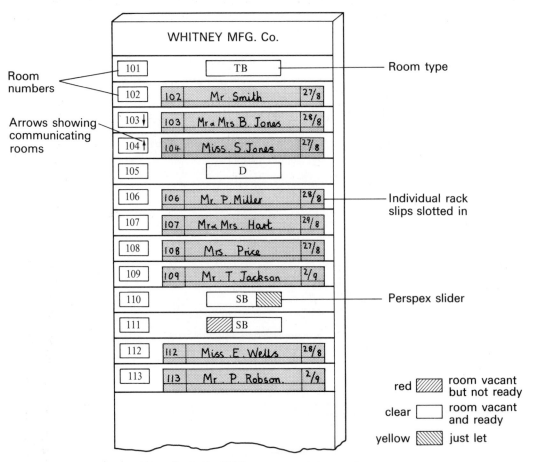

Part of a Whitney room status rack

Accurate information on room status throughout the hotel is most important, of course. A room status system must provide clear information and it must be capable of rapid alteration. There are various methods in use from simple manual systems such as the room board to computerized systems such as electronic room status linking reception, housekeeping, and the cashier's office.

1 What kind of information is requested on registration cards?
2 Why must the receptionist check completed registration forms?
3 What should the receptionist obtain from a guest with a travel agency booking?
4 Why is it useful for a tour leader to deal with the registration cards for a tour group?
5 Give three examples of room status systems.

Listen to the dialogue on your cassette before you read it in your book. Try to understand the meanings of any new words or expressions while you are listening to the dialogue. After that, look for new words and expressions in the Word Study at the end of the unit.

Mr John Rawson has arrived in Naples. While you are listening to his conversation with Maria Leone, one of the receptionists at the Hotel Plaza, fill in the Key Card below.

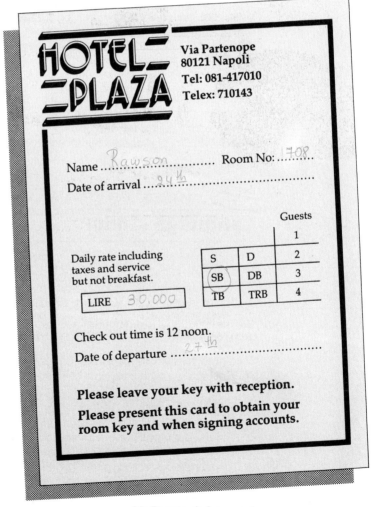

Mr Rawson's key card

Leone Good evening. Can I help you?

Rawson Yes. I've booked a room for the next three nights.

Leone Could you give me your name, please?

Rawson Yes. It's Rawson. John Rawson.

Leone Ah yes, Mr Rawson. Here it is. A single with bath until the 27th. Would you fill in this Registration Card while I prepare your Key Card?

Rawson Certainly. Ah good, it's in English. Let me see … name … first name … Why do you need these passport details?

Leone They are for the Police Department. We have to ask you for this information by law.

Rawson Here you are. I think I've filled it in correctly.

Leone Yes, that's fine, Mr Rawson. Here's your key. It's room 708 on the seventh floor and the daily rate is 30,000 lire, excluding breakfast.

And here's your Key Card with details of your booking on the front. Inside, it tells you about all the services the hotel can provide. You should carry it at all times. You'll need it as identification in the hotel's bars and restaurants if you want drinks and meals charged to your account.

Rawson Right. I'll take good care of that. You mentioned food. Is it possible to get something to eat this late?

Leone Yes, our Belvedere restaurant is still open. Or if you want something lighter, there's the Coffee Shop. It's open round the clock.

Rawson Good. I'll put my luggage in my room first. How do I get to it?

Leone Don't worry about that. The porter will take your bags up in the lift and show you to your room.

Rawson Right. Thank you very much. Good night.

Listening check

1 Why should Mr Rawson carry his Key Card?
2 At what time of the day did Mr Rawson arrive?
3 When does the Coffee Shop close?
4 How will Mr Rawson find his room?

Language study

Asking questions

Examples:

Find out if he requires a room with bath.
▶ Do you require a room with bath, sir?

You don't know if Mrs Thomas has made a reservation.
▶ Have you made a reservation, Mrs Thomas?

Find out when Mr Harris confirmed his booking.
▶ When did you confirm your booking, Mr Harris?

Now do the following in a similar way.

1 You want to know if Mr Jones can change his booking.
2 Find out if she will confirm in writing.
3 You want to know if Mr Laker is cancelling his reservation.
4 You want to know which tour group he is with.
5 You need to know where his next destination is.
6 You don't know if the tour group has arrived.
7 Find out if the receptionist checked the registration card.

8 You need to know who Mrs Masters is waiting for.
9 Find out why Mr Qatan is leaving earlier than expected.
10 You need to know if he wants an early call.

Describing people's jobs

Example:

What is a receptionist?

▶ A person **who/that** works in reception.

Now complete the following.

1 What is an enquiry clerk?   ▶ ......
2 ......   ▶ A person that deals with reservation enquiries.
3 What is a hotel porter?   ▶ ......
4 ......   ▶ A person who sells holidays.
5 What is a clerk?   ▶ ......
6 What is a book-keeper?   ▶ ......

Nations, nationalities and currency

Complete the following table.

nation	nationality	currency
1 France	FRENCH	Fr
2 Spain	Spanish	Pta
3 Britain	British	£
4 Italy	Italian	L
5 Greece	Greek	Dr
6 Denmark	Danish	D Kr
7 Netherland	Dutch	Guilder
8 Switzerland	Swiss	S Fr
9 Germany	German	DM
10 Japan	Japanese	Y
11 U.S.A.	American	$
12 Mexico	Mexican	P
13 Sweden	Swedish	SeK
14 Austria	Austrian	Sch
15 Belgium	Belgian	Fr
16 Portugal	Portuguese	Esc

Fr is the **abbreviation** for franc. Find out the full forms for the currency abbreviations in the table.

Advising

Notice how we use **should** when we are giving advice.

Examples:

The receptionist didn't check the registration cards.
▶ You **should** always check the registration cards.

The guest left his Key Card in his room.
▶ You **should** always carry your Key Card.

In a similar way, use **should** for the following sentences.

1 The receptionist didn't prepare the arrival list.
2 The guest forgot his Hotel Voucher.
3 The clerk forgot to confirm a booking.
4 The receptionist was not polite to the guests.
5 The reservations clerk didn't note down the customer's name.

Listening and Speaking

Listening

Maria Leone is busy dealing with guests' queries. While you are listening to the four dialogues, decide if the following statements are true (T) or false (F). There are two statements for each dialogue. Remember, don't read the dialogues in your book or look in the Word Study until you have listened to them on the cassette.

1 Mrs Grant thought that her room was too noisy.   T/F
2 Maria Leone will give Mrs Grant a new Key Card.   T/F
3 Mr Rawson may have to change rooms for the last night.   T/F
4 If you dial 9, you get an external line.   T/F
5 Mr Blunt's double rooms should be adjoining. *together*   T/F
6 Mr Blunt wants to be near his eighty-year-old parents.   T/F
7 Peter Jackson is staying in room 804.   T/F
8 Mr Blakeson needn't ring the Diplomat if he is able to be at the meeting.   T/F

Dialogue 1

Grant Good morning. My name's Grant. I'm in room 204.

Leone Good morning, Mrs Grant. What can I do for you?

Grant Well, I don't want to make any trouble but I'm not happy with my room. I didn't sleep at all last night.

Leone Oh dear, I'm sorry to hear that.

Grant Yes, there was a lot of noise from the street. It seemed to go on all night.

Leone Well, I'll see if I can find another, quieter, room for you. ... Yes, 613 is vacant. It's higher up and at the back of the hotel. If you have your bags ready, the porter will collect them and show you where the room is.

Grant That's very good of you.

Leone If you bring your Key Card to reception, I'll change the room number on it.

Grant Thank you. I'll do that.

Dialogue 2

Leone Reception. Good morning.

Rawson Good morning. This is Mr Rawson in 708. My company has been in touch with me this morning. They'd like me to stay on here in Naples for two more days. I wonder if it's possible to extend my stay here until the 29th?

Leone Would you hold the line, Mr Rawson? I'll check the booking situation. ... Yes, that will be all right. It may be necessary to ask you to change rooms for the last night. Would that be acceptable?

Rawson Yes, that's no problem. There is one other thing, too. There's no information in my room about making external calls. I'm trying to call a Pescara number.

Leone I'm sorry there's no information. I'll ask Housekeeping to check it. If you dial 9, you'll get an outside line. The Pescara area code is 085.

Rawson Fine. Thanks for your help.

Dialogue 3

Blunt Blunt's the name. I have a reservation for tonight.

Leone Good evening, Mr Blunt. Let me see. Two doubles for one night. Numbers 602 and 714.

Blunt Are they on different floors, then?

Leone Yes, in fact they are.

Blunt They should be together. I booked two adjoining doubles. We're travelling with my wife's parents and they're both over 80. It's absolutely necessary that we are near them.

Leone I'm sorry, sir. If you'd like to take a seat for a few minutes, I'll see what I can do. I'm sure it won't take long.

Blunt I certainly hope not.

Leone Would you excuse me?

Dialogue 4

Leone Reception. Can I help you?

Smith Yes, my name's Smith. I'm trying to contact Peter Blakeson. I think he's staying in 804.

Leone Yes, he is. I'll try his extension for you. . . . I'm sorry. There's no answer from 804. Can I take a message for him?

Smith Yes, please. I'm Chuck Smith of Offshore Oil Services Inc. I'd like Mr Blakeson to meet me tomorrow evening in the cocktail bar at the Hotel Diplomat on Via Garibaldi between 7 and 7.30. If he can make the appointment, he doesn't need to contact me. If he can't, he should ring me at the Diplomat this evening before 8. He knows the number. Have you got all that?

Leone Yes. I'll make sure that Mr Blakeson gets the message.

Speaking
Asking questions

Study the following examples.

Head receptionist Ask Mr Jones if he requires an early morning call.
Receptionist *Do you require an early morning call, Mr Jones?*

Head receptionist Ask Mrs Smith if she has completed her form.
Receptionist *Have you completed the form, Mrs Smith?*

Now do the exercise on the tape, forming questions in a similar way. After you speak you will hear the receptionist's words on the tape.

Activities

Activity A

In the first Listening section, you heard Mr Rawson checking in at the Hotel Plaza. Use the information in that dialogue and the Reading section to supply the missing information on the Registration Form for Mr Rawson on the next page.

REGISTRATION CARD

HOTEL PLAZA

Name	RAWSON
First Names	JOHN
1	BRITISH

3 VISITORS

2

4 L 493677 B

55, NORTH HILL, WANDSWORTH
LONDON SW18 2QZ, ENGLAND

5

LIVERPOOL

FREE RESERVATION SERVICE
Travelling on to other places in the U.K. & Europe?
Please ask the receptionist if we can help make
your reservation

6 Address

HOTEL PATRAS

SYNTAGMA SQUARE

ATHENS · GREECE

7 *J. Rawson*

Room No.	No. of Persons	Charge	Date of Arrival	No. of Nights or Departure Date	
8	**9**	**10**	**11**	27· 8· 82	

Mr Rawson's registration card

<table>
<tr><td>

Activity B

</td><td>

A guest who stays at a hotel without an advance booking is often
called a 'chance' guest. Receptionists have little information about
these guests. There are different ways of deciding whether to accept
chance arrivals or not. How do you think an hotel should deal with the
problem?

</td></tr>
<tr><td>

Activity C

</td><td>

Use the information in the following description of the Whitney room
status system to complete the flow chart opposite.

When a guest checks in, the receptionist looks at the room rack and
allocates a room by pushing the slider to yellow. This shows that the
room is let. After the guest has registered, the receptionist prepares a
rack slip. These rack slips are normally in four parts: in white, pink,
yellow, and blue. The white copy is placed in the room slot, the pink
copy goes into the alphabetical rack, the yellow copy goes to the
telephonist and the blue copy goes to the porter's desk. This system
makes sure that the house list is kept in alphabetical order.

When a guest leaves, the rack slip is removed from the room rack
and crossed through with a red pencil. This is then sent to the other
departments and the staff remove the guest's slip. In this way, the
house list is still kept in alphabetical order.

</td></tr>
</table>

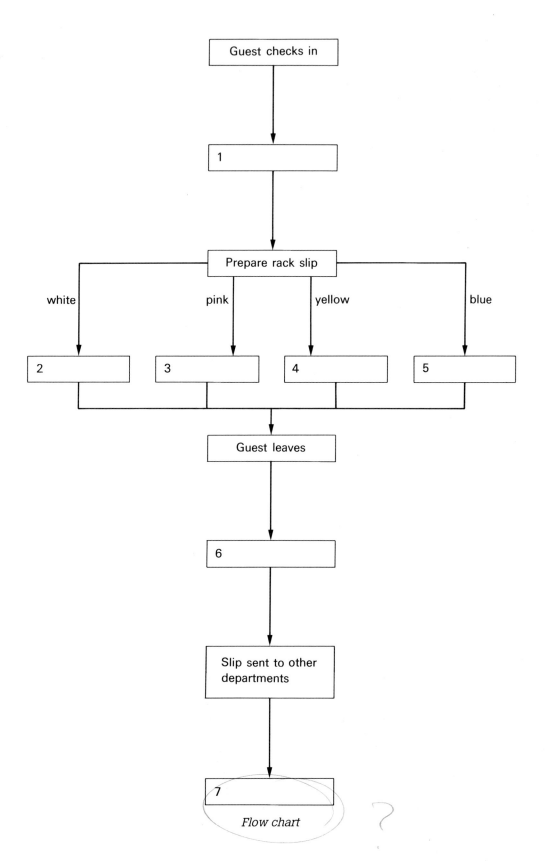

Guest checks in

1

Prepare rack slip

white   pink   yellow   blue

2   3   4   5

Guest leaves

6

Slip sent to other departments

7

Flow chart

Writing

The Hotel Adriatico in Brindisi has received this letter.

```
                                        23 Burley Lodge Road
                                        Nottingham
                                        England


                                        17 March 1982

The Manager
Hotel Adriatico
Piazza Rumboldi
Brindiai
Italy

Dear Sir,
A few weeks ago, I booked a double room and a single room
in your hotel.  The dates were from 18 to 25 June.
Unfortunately, my father has been very ill recently and
his doctor has ordered complete rest for six months.  He
will not, therefore, accompany my wife and me on our
journey to Italy.  For this reason, we would like to cancel
the single room.  My wife and I still plan to arrive as
arranged.

Yours faithfully,


William Bond
```

Here is the reply from the Hotel Adriatico.

Hotel Adriatico

Piazza Rumboldi ● Brindisi ● Italia ●
Telefono 0831-23418 ● Telex 861178 ●

Mr William Bond
23 Burley Lodge Road
Nottingham
England

11 April 1982

Dear Mr Bond,

Thank you for your letter of 17 March 1982.

We are sorry to hear that your father is ill and hope that he will
soon recover.

We have, as you requested, cancelled the single reservation and are
now holding for you one double room with bath for the period 18-25
June.

Yours sincerely,

Mr P Menotti
Advance Reservations

Using Mr Menotti's letter as an example, write letters of reply to the
following requests for alterations to bookings. You can accept all of
these changes.

1 William Cook, 1976 Gulf Boulevard, Indian Rocks, Florida, U.S.A.
   Original booking: T/B, from 22 July, 6 nights, arriving 15.00.
   Change: arriving 23 July at 17.00, still require 6 nights

2 Eva Pettersson, Tideliusgatan 53, S-351 39 Kalmar, Sweden
   Original booking: 2D, from 14 August, 8 nights
   Change: leaving on 20th, please confirm booking for 6 nights

3 Jack Archer, 49 Methuen Way, Edgeware, Middlesex, England
   Original Booking: S/B, from 29 June, 2 nights
   Change: change of plans, please cancel booking.

Word study

accompany p. 30, travel with.

accurate p. 22, correct.

additional p. 21, extra.

adjoining p. 27, next to each other.

alteration p. 22, change. v alter.

area code p. 26, telephone number for a part of the country.

charged to ... account p. 24, put on ... bill.

check against p. 22, compare with.

checking in p. 22, registering.

clarification p. 22, extra information to make something clear. v clarify.

cocktail bar p. 27, bar for drinks before dinner.

destination p. 22, place to which a person is going.

excluding p. 24, the opposite of 'including'.

extend p. 26, make longer.

extension p. 27, internal telephone number.

external calls p. 26, calls to numbers outside the hotel.

fill in p. 24, complete.

hotel register p. 21, book in which information about guests is recorded.

hotel voucher p. 22, form issued by travel agent reserving hotel accommodation and often recording part of full payment in advance.

identification p. 24, way of showing who you are. A passport, for example, identifies who you are.

in touch p. 26, in contact.

legibly p. 22, in a way that is easily read.

let p. 28, occupied; rented.

lift p. 24, (US) elevator.

manual p. 22, hand-operated.

mentioned p. 24, spoke about.

method of payment p. 22, way of paying.

obtain p. 22, get.

open round the clock p. 24, open 24 hours a day.

original p. 31, first.

outside line p. 26, telephone line going out from hotel.

place of issue p. 21, place where passport was obtained.

provide p. 21, give; supply.

purpose of visit p. 22, reason for visit.

query p. 22, question.

recently p. 30, not long ago.

room status p. 22, condition and availability of each room.

room board p. 22, board showing room status.

signature p. 21, v sign.

therefore p. 30, because of this; for this reason.

tour groups p. 22, groups of people travelling and staying in hotels under one booking.

tour leader p. 22, person in charge of a tour group.

travel agency p. 22, place where travel agent works.

vacant p. 26, free; unoccupied.

various p. 22, different; a number of. v vary; n variety.

Unit 3
Hotel services

Reading and Listening

Here is a list of services described in the Key Card of the Patras Hotel. Remember not to look in the Word Study until after you have read the passage.

Welcome to the
PATRAS HOTEL

 ROOM SERVICE For everything you want, please use the telephone in your room. Breakfast only is served in the bedrooms.

 TEA AND COFFEE There are tea and coffee making facilities in all the bedrooms.

 NIGHT PORTER The Night Porter has a supply of drinks if you need something after the bar has closed and he is on call throughout the night.

22.00 – 07.00

 CAR PARKING The hotel car park is available to all guests, but we regret that no responsibility can be taken for cars left in the car park.

 SHOE CLEANING SERVICE There are shoe cleaning machines on the second and fifth floors.

 LAUNDRY A same-day service is available Monday to Friday. Garments handed to the Hall Porter before 10 a.m. will be returned the same evening.

 DOCTOR In an emergency, private medical attention can be obtained by contacting the Housekeeper, Reception Office or the Duty Manager.

 THEATRE TICKETS These can be obtained by contacting Reception.

 TRANSPORT For car hire, travel information and taxi service, please contact Reception or the Hall Porter.

 VALUABLES Valuables should be deposited at the Reception Office and a receipt obtained for them. Otherwise, the Management cannot accept responsibility.

 CHEQUES The Reception Office will arrange for the changing of foreign currency and will cash traveller's cheques. Personal cheques will be cashed at the Management's discretion.

FIRE INSTRUCTIONS
Please read the Fire Notice on display in your room.

1 Which meals are not served in a guest's bedroom?
2 Who cleans guests' shoes?
3 Who is responsible for cash kept in a guest's bedroom?
4 Who should be contacted in a medical emergency?
5 Where are the fire instructions situated?

Listening

Karina Stelios is <u>on duty in the Reception</u> of the Patras Hotel when she is phoned by a worried person. Remember, don't read the dialogues in your book or look in the Word Study until you have listened to them on the cassette.

First Call

Fairfax Hello. Reception? This is Mrs Fairfax in 219. We have an urgent problem. Is there a doctor in the hotel?

Stelios No, I'm afraid there isn't. But we can call one quickly in an emergency. Aren't you feeling well?

Fairfax It's not me. It's my husband. He has very bad pains in his chest.

Stelios <u>I'll call the doctor at once. Can you describe any more symptoms?</u>

Fairfax Yes, his breathing is weak, but he doesn't seem to have a temperature. It looks as if he's had a heart attack.

Stelios Right. <u>I'll get in touch with the doctor immediately</u> and pass that information on to him. I'll call you back as soon as I know what he can do.

Second Call

Stelios Hello, Mrs Fairfax. The doctor said that he'd be here within twenty minutes. He said that your husband's clothes should be loosened and that he should be kept warm.

Fairfax Yes, I'll do that. You'll send the doctor up as soon as he comes?

Stelios Yes, of course I will, Mrs Fairfax.

Fairfax About the fee? Do I have to pay the doctor in cash when he comes?

Stelios Don't worry about that now. He is a private doctor so it will be necessary to pay, but we'll arrange all that later.

Third Call

Fairfax This is Mrs Fairfax from 219 again. Thank you for getting the doctor so quickly. He gave my husband some drugs and he seems much better now. He also left a prescription, and said that the medicine should be taken three times a day. The problem is that I can't leave my husband.

Stelios <u>We'll take care of the prescription</u>, Mrs Fairfax. <u>I'll send a porter up to your room.</u> He'll collect the prescription and take it to the chemist's straight away.

Fairfax That's very kind of you. Thank you.

Listening check

1 What is wrong with Mr Fairfax?
2 What are the symptoms?
3 What should Mrs Fairfax do before the doctor arrives?
4 When will Mrs Fairfax have to pay the doctor's bill?
5 Why is the porter going to room 219?

Language study

Study the following examples of a receptionist passing on the messages of different guests.

'Tell my husband that **I'll wait** for **him** in the bar,' said Mrs Law.
▶ 'Your wife said **she would wait** for **you** in the bar, Mr Law.'

'Tell Mr Lutz that **I am arriving** at six o'clock,' said Mr Logan.
▶ 'Mr Logan said that **he was arriving** at six o'clock, Mr Lutz.'

'Could you tell the Duty Manager **I want** to see **him**?' said Mr Jones.
▶ 'Mr Jones said **he wanted** to see **you**, sir.'

In a similar way, report the following messages, taking care to make changes where they are necessary.

1 'Tell Mr Graham that I have a message for him,' said Mrs Betts.
2 'Would you inform the housekeeper that I need some soap?' said Mr Tor.
3 'Could you tell my husband that I'll see him in the lobby?' said Mrs Reid.
4 'Tell my wife I'm going to the shops,' said Mr Parks.
5 'Tell the tour leader we need the registration cards,' said the manager.
6 'Could you tell the cashier I want my bill?' said Peter Jones.
7 'Tell my wife that I have collected the newspaper,' said Mr Lambert.
8 'Tell Mrs Pritchard that I'm leaving at two,' said her sister.

Using nouns in groups

Examples:

reservation chart   ▶ chart for recording reservations
booking confirmation   ▶ confirmation of a booking

Now complete the following in a similar way.

1 tea making facilities   ▶ ......
2 tour group leader   ▶ ......
3 ......   ▶ service provided in a guest's room
4 ......   ▶ system for reserving airline seats
5 shoe cleaning machine   ▶ ......
6 ......   ▶ telephone code for an area
7 ......   ▶ bureau which finds accommodation
8 ......   ▶ form for registering guests from overseas
9 arrival list   ▶ ......
10 room status system   ▶ ......

Guests, please 1 deposit valuables at Reception.
                  2 order newspapers at the desk.
                  3 sign registration cards on arrival.
                  4 confirm reservations in writing.
                  5 change traveller's cheques at the cash desk.
                  6 leave your keys at Reception.

Note how we can use a Passive form to write out the first example above:

Valuables **should be deposited** at Reception.

Note that it is not necessary to speak about the guests.

Use **can, should** and **must** to write Passive sentences for examples 2–6.

Listening and Speaking

Karina Stelios is on duty in Reception again. While you are listening to her conversations and telephone calls, complete the table below. Remember, don't read the dialogues in your book or look in the Word Study until you have listened to them on the cassette.

Message	From	Room	To	Room	Request/Action
1	MR HURST				
2					Has urgent business meeting. Wait in Capital Bar until past 4.
3			ROOM SERVICE		
4		219			

Dialogue 1

Guest Good evening. My name's Hurst. I'm in room 200.

Stelios Good evening, Mr Hurst. What can I do for you?

Guest I'd like an early call tomorrow morning, please.

Stelios Certainly. When would you like us to call you?

Guest I'm not sure. I have to be at the West Terminal, Hellenikon Airport for an eight o'clock flight. When should I leave here, do you think?

Stelios The minimum check-in time is sixty minutes, so you need to arrive at the airport by seven. If you get a taxi from here at 6.15 you'll be absolutely sure of getting there on time.

Guest OK. I'll have a 5.30 call, please.

Stelios Right, Mr Hurst. Good night.

Guest Good night.

Dialogue 2

Guest Hello, I'm from room 370. My name's John Steel. Could you do something for me?

Stelios Yes, I hope so, Mr Steel.

Guest The situation is this: a friend of mine is coming here at about three. I asked him to meet me here, in fact. The problem is that I have to go to an urgent business meeting and I won't be back until after four. I've tried ringing him but there's no answer. Could you ask him to wait for me in the Capital Bar?

Stelios Yes, of course. what is his name?

Guest Mr Pettersson. He's from Sweden. I'll spell the name for you. P-E-double T-E-R-double S-O-N.

Stelios Right, Mr Steel. I'll see that he gets your message.

Dialogue 3

Guest Good morning. I wonder if you could tell me when the banks are open today.

Stelios I'm afraid they're closed all day today. It's a public holiday.

Guest That's a nuisance. I'm a little short of cash. I do have some traveller's cheques with me and my credit cards, too. Could you help me?

Stelios That's no problem. Traveller's cheques can be cashed here in the hotel. The Cashier will help you with those. And your credit cards will be accepted in many shops, restaurants, and night clubs.

Guest Fine. I'll cash some cheques now. Oh, there is one other thing. My wife is in bed with a headache. I think it's all this sun. Would you ask Room Service to send us some hot milk and a few aspirins?

Stelios Yes, sir. I'll make sure that you get them soon. Your room number is . . .?

Guest 342. Thank you very much.

Dialogue 4

Stelios Reception. Can I help you?

Guest This is Mrs Fairfax from 219.

Stelios Ah, hello, Mrs Fairfax. I was on duty when your husband fell ill. How is he now?

Guest He's much better, thank you, but still weak. The doctor said he needed a complete check-up and then a long rest. We're going back to Britain sooner than we planned. That's why I'm calling you. We're booked on a midday flight next Wednesday. Now we'd like to leave on Saturday and earlier in the day if possible. We have a long drive from London Airport. Could you help us with the bookings?

Stelios Certainly. I'll see what can be done, Mrs Fairfax. Would you let me have your tickets when you're passing Reception?

Guest Yes, of course.

Study the following examples.

Mrs Betts I'm Mrs Betts. Would you tell Mr Graham that I have a
message for him?
Receptionist *Mrs Betts said that she had a message for you, Mr
Graham.*

Mr Tor This is Mr Tor in 802. Would you inform the Housekeeper that I
need some soap?
Receptionist *Mr Tor, in 802, said that he wanted some soap.*

Now do the exercise on the tape, reporting messages in a similar way.
After you speak, you will hear the receptionist's words on the tape.

Activities

Activity A

Hotel guests have a wide variety of needs. Some of these are listed
below. Decide which member, or members, of staff should deal with
each of these requirements. For example, if a guest wanted   a. some
drinks in his room, he could call   6 the Night Porter or   9 Room
Service.

A guest wants:

a. some drinks in his room
b. some soap
c. to stay at the hotel again
d. his shirts cleaned
e. some writing paper
f. to leave a message
g. to cash a traveller's cheque
h. to extend her stay
i. some theatre tickets
j. medical attention
k. to hire a car
l. to change her room
m. to cash a personal cheque
n. to deposit some valuables
o. an early call
p. a newspaper in his room
q. his baggage moved

Members of staff

1 Bookings Clerk
2 Cashier
3 Duty Manager
4 Hall Porter
5 Housekeeper
6 Night Porter
7 Porter
8 Receptionist
9 Room Service

Activity B

In one of the Listening dialogues, you heard that Mr and Mrs Fairfax
would like to go back to Britain on Saturday and on an earlier flight
than OA 259. Look at the timetable below and decide which flight is
best for them.

Service	Dep	Arr	Fl No	Acft	Cl	St
From ATHENS Greece (ATH) To LONDON UK (LON)		LHR – Heathrow		LGW – Gatwick		
6	0505	0805 LHR	KQ 514	707	FY	1
6	0525	0825 LHR	KQ 514	707	FY	1
2	0635	0810 LHR	SQ 75	747	FY	0
4	0920	1205 LGW	OA 261	707	Y	1
1 345 7	0930	1105 LHR	BA 561	L10	FY	0
2 6	0930	1105 LHR	BA 561	TRD	FY	0
1234567	1155	1335 LHR	OA 259	AB3	FY	0
6	1650	1830 LGW	KU 191	707	FY	0

Key

Service
1 = Monday
2 = Tuesday
3 = Wednesday
4 = Thursday
etc.

Dep = Departure
Arr = Arrival
Fl No = flight number
Acft = type of aircraft
Cl = class
St = number of stops

F = first class
Y = economy class

Part of the London-Athens schedule (adapted) ABC Airlines Guide

Now answer these questions about the timetable.

1 How many daily flights are there to London?
2 Why is OA 261 slower than BA 561?
3 How many non-stop flights are there on Saturdays?
4 How many of the flights carry first class passengers?
5 How many airlines fly Athens–London non-stop?
6 Non-stop flights take about 2½ hours. How much is British time behind Greek time?

Writing

A receptionist at the Patras Hotel has taken three messages.

Here are her notes.

- Mr Powers/arriving Hellenikon Airport/7 pm today
  take taxi/meet Mr Long here
- Mrs Sampson/gone shopping/back midday
  meet husband for lunch/Belvedere Restaurant/1 pm
- Mr Peters/room 702/checked out/7 am/day early
  booked in Linda Kemp/chance arrival/702/one night only

And here are the three messages written out in full. Compare the notes with the full messages.

- Mr Powers is arriving at Hellenikon Airport at 7 pm today. He will take a taxi and meet Mr Long here at the hotel.
- Mrs Sampson has gone shopping and she will be back at midday. She will meet her husband for lunch in the Belvedere Restaurant at 1 pm.
- Mr Peters, room 702, checked out at 7 am, a day early. I have booked in Linda Kemp, a chance arrival, in room 702 for one night only.

Writing B

Now cover the three messages. Look at the notes again and try to write out the messages in full yourself.

Writing C

Write out the following messages in full.

1 Mr Brown/leaving/3 pm/this afternoon
   catch flight/London/Hellenikon Airport/6 pm
2 Mrs Curtis/ordered taxi/10.30 am
   meet brother/entrance to Akropolis/11.00 am
3 Miss Wiseman/cancelled order/'Times' newspaper
   changed order/'International Herald Tribune'
4 Mr Drew/made booking/21.3.82/3 nights/SB
   sent letter/confirming booking
5 Mrs Payne/called doctor/9 am/husband ill
   doctor/sent Mr Payne/City Hospital/11 am
6 John Adams/left message/Mr Authur/midday
   not able to meet/Diplomat Bar/7 pm/this evening

Word study

baggage p. 39, luggage.
car hire p. 34, use of a car for payment.
cash p. 34, change into money. Cash is also another word for money.
chemist p. 35, shop where medicines are obtained.
cheque p. 34

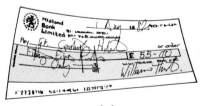

personal cheque

credit card p. 38

traveller's cheque

currency p. 34, money.
deposited p. 34, given for safe
  keeping.
discretion p. 34, freedom to decide.
drugs p. 35, medicines.
duty manager p. 34, manager made
  responsible for day to day
  operations.
emergency p. 34, problem which .
  requires immediate attention.
facilities p. 34, equipment.
fee p. 35, charge.
fire notice p. 34, instructions on what
  to do if there is a fire.
flight p. 38, airline journey.
garments p. 34, pieces of clothing.
headache p. 38, pain in the head.
heart attack p. 35, sudden illness of
  the heart.
loosened p. 35, made free; undone.
on call p. 34, available for contact.
on display p. 34, put where it can be
  seen.
on time p. 38, at the correct time.

otherwise p. 34, if not.
prescription p. 35, written note used
  for obtaining medicine.
public holiday p. 38, national holiday
  such as May 1st or December 25th.
  In the UK, the expression 'bank
  holiday' is also used.
receipt p. 34, written note recording
  money or valuables received.
regret p. 34, are sorry.
responsible for p. 35, in charge of;
  accountable for.
same-day service p. 34, service
  which is completed on the same
  day it is requested.
situated p. 35, placed; sited; located.
straight away p. 35, immediately.
symptoms p. 35, signs of illness.
throughout p. 34, all through.
urgent p. 35, requiring immediate
  attention.
valuables p. 34, things worth a lot of
  money.
within p. 35, before the end of.

1	bandages	5	pills
2	plasters	6	medicine bottle
3	scissors	7	cotton wool
4	safety pins	8	thermometer

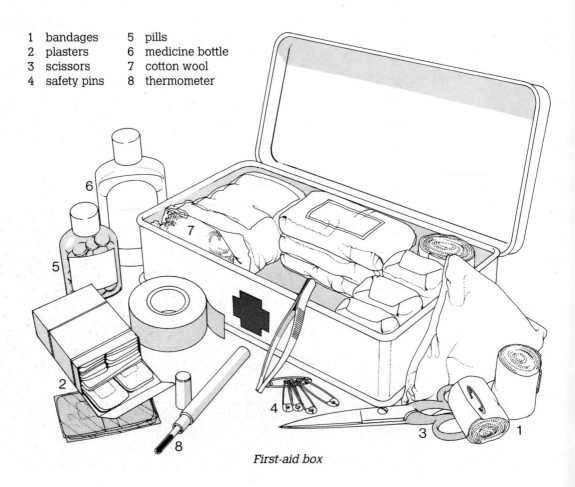

First-aid box

Unit 4
Food service 1

Reading and Listening

Here is part of the introduction to the Good Eating Guide for France 1982. Remember not to look in the Word Study until after you have read the passage.

CLASSIFICATION

A large number of restaurants are mentioned in this guide. We particularly recommend some of them for the high quality of their cuisine. These establishments are indicated by Good Eating Stars. For each of the starred restaurants, we have also shown three speciality dishes which are usually served à la carte. Some of these dishes are available only in season.

★   A *good restaurant* where carefully prepared meals are served at reasonable prices.

★★   A *very good restaurant* where first-rate cuisine is available.

★★★   An *excellent restaurant* where the very best food and wines are served.

PRICES OF MEALS

The rates for each restaurant give an indication of basic charges current in Spring 1982. Prices are given in francs and are inclusive of service and VAT. If you think that an establishment has overcharged you, let us know.

M 50/140   **Fixed price meals** – A minimum of 50 and a maximum of 140 francs for set meals served at normal eating hours.

b.i.   Beverage included.

M à la c   **A la carte meals** – The first amount is for a plain but 80/180   well-prepared meal which includes a light entrée, a main dish of the day with vegetables, and a dessert or cheese. The second figure is for a fuller meal with a house speciality and includes hors d'oeuvres, two main courses, cheese and a dessert.

[handwritten margin note: STARTER]

Reading check

1 What kinds of restaurants does the Good Eating Guide recommend?
2 What is the difference between a one star and a two star restaurant?
3 What does the basic charge include?
4 Is a beverage always included in the set meals?
5 How many courses are served in the cheaper à la carte meal?

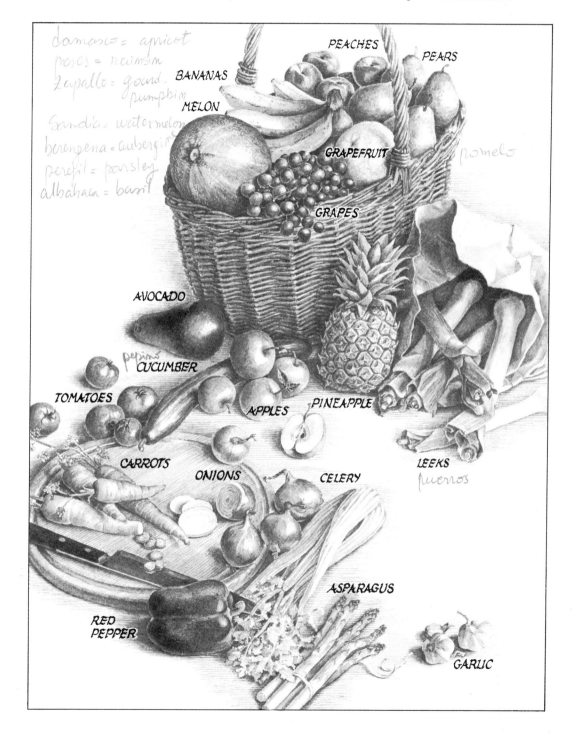

damasco = apricot
poros = racimsin
zapallo = gourd.
   pumpkin
Sandia = watermelon
berengena = aubergine
perejil = parsley
albahaca = basil

PEACHES
PEARS
BANANAS
MELON
pomelo
GRAPEFRUIT
GRAPES
AVOCADO
pepino
CUCUMBER
TOMATOES
APPLES   PINEAPPLE
CARROTS   ONIONS   CELERY
LEEKS
puerros
RED PEPPER
ASPARAGUS
GARLIC

Two customers have entered the restaurant of the Hotel Prince. While you are listening to the dialogue, look at the menu below. Remember, don't read the dialogue in your book or look in the Word Study until you have listened to it on the cassette.

Menu à 120 francs

Les hors d'oeuvres

Les poissons

Filets de Macquereaux au Vin Blanc
(Mackerel fillets in white wine)

Sole Normande
(Sole in cream and cider sauce)

Les viandes

Sauté de Boeuf Chasseur
(Beef with wine and mushrooms)

Steak au Poivre
(Pepper steak)

Noisettes Milanese
(Lamb served with spaghetti)

Les légumes

Petits pois
(Peas)

Endives au beurre
(Chicory in butter)

Pommes de terre Anna
(Potatoes in butter)

Les fromages

Les désserts

Crème à l'orange
(Orange cream)

Tarte aux abricots
(Apricot tart)

Mousse au chocolat
(Chocolate mousse)

Reception waiter Good evening, sir.

Mr Carson Good evening. My name is Carson. I've booked a table for two for nine o'clock.

Reception waiter Ah, Mr Carson. That's right, a table for two. Would you come this way, please?

Station waiter Good evening. Would you like to take your seats, gentlemen?

Mr Carson Thank you.

Mr James Thank you very much.

Station waiter Would you like an apéritif before you order?

Mr Carson No, I think we'd like to order straight away.

Station waiter Your menus.

Mr Carson Thank you. Now let's see ...

Station waiter Have you decided yet, sir?

Mr Carson No, I'm still looking at the menu. Tell me, what would you recommend for the main course?

Station waiter Why don't you try the beef chasseur? It's very good.

Mr Carson Fine. I'll have the beef.

Station waiter And to start?

Mr Carson I'll have the hors d'oeuvres and then the sole. What about you, John?

Mr James I don't like beef very much. What is noisettes Milanese exactly?

Station waiter That's lamb cooked with herbs and served with spaghetti.

Mr James That sounds interesting. I'll try that. And I'll start with the hors d'oeuvres followed by the mackerel.

Station waiter Very good, sir. And vegetables?

Mr Carson I'll have peas and potatoes.

Mr James Just chicory for me, please.

Station waiter Thank you very much.

Wine waiter Good evening, gentlemen. Your wine list.

Mr Carson Right. Let's have a look. ... What about a Chablis to start with, John?

Mr James Yes, that suits me fine.

Mr Carson Bring us a half bottle of Chablis to begin with, and then I think we'll try the Beaujolais.

Wine waiter Very good, sir.

Listening check

1 What dish does the waiter recommend for the main course?
2 What does Mr James order for his first two courses?
3 Who orders the noisettes Milanese?
4 How is noisettes Milanese served?
5 Which wines does Mr Carson order?

Language study

Making suggestions

Study the following table.

situation	suggestion
1 You are eating fish	a Chablis
2 You feel hungry	the English breakfast
3 You're looking for a good restaurant	the Good Eating Guide
4 You have a headache	an aspirin
5 It's a long way to walk	a taxi
6 You feel very hot	a beer
7 You've had a tiring day	a rest

Notice how we can make suggestions for 1.

> If you are eating fish, madam/sir, **I'd suggest**
> a Chablis.
>
> **or** If you are eating fish, madam/sir, **why don't you try**
> a Chablis?
>
> **or** If you are eating fish, madam/sir **what about trying**
> a Chablis?

POLITER

In a similar way, use the table to make suggestions for 2–7.

Describing dishes and drinks

Example:

What's noisettes Milanese exactly? (Cook lamb with herbs and serve it with spaghetti.)
▶ That's lamb cooked with herbs and served with spaghetti.

In a similar way, describe the following.

1 What's a dry Martini? (Mix three parts gin with one part dry Martini and serve it with an olive.)
2 Could you tell me what paella is? (Cook rice and sea food together and serve it in the cooking dish.)
3 What's blanquette of veal? (Cook veal with carrots and onions and serve it in a white sauce with boiled rice.)
4 Could you explain what an Irish coffee is? (Mix coffee with brown sugar, Irish whiskey, and cream, and serve it as an after-dinner drink.)
5 What's sweet and sour pork? (Fry pieces of pork and serve in a sugar and vinegar sauce with rice.)

Present time

Notice how the Present Perfect and the Present Continuous are used in the examples.

Examples:

Have you decided yet, sir? (look at/menu)
▶ No, I haven't. I'm still looking at the menu.

No, he hasn't. I'm still waiting for him. (brother/arrive)
▶ Has your brother arrived?

In a similar way, make questions or answers for the following.

1 Have you ordered yet? (wait for/menu)
2 Have you found your wallet? (look for)
3 No, it hasn't. We're still waiting for it. ('Times'/arrive)
4 No, I haven't. I'm still waiting for a line. (telephone/company)
5 No, I haven't. I'm still filling it in. (complete/registration form)
6 Have you finished with the tour guide? (use)
7 No, I haven't. I'm still waiting for confirmation. (allocate/tour group)
8 Have you prepared the room? (clean)

Listening and Speaking

Guests in the Hôtel de France are ordering food and drinks in the bar, in the coffee shop, and by telephone. While you are listening to the dialogues, note down the orders on an order pad like the one below. Remember, don't read the dialogues in your book or look in the Word Study until you have listened to them on the cassette.

HOTEL DE FRANCE Nice

Order Pad (Food and Beverage Service)

Order *1 orange juice* | *fresh*
1 grape fruit j.
1 bacon - egg - tomato
2 softed boiled eggs
toast - butter - merm.
tea with lemon

Notes *7.30*

Name *Mr & Mrs Sand*

Room *226*   Date

Order form

Dialogue 1

Guest Hello, Room Service. This is room 226. We'd like to order breakfast for tomorrow.

Floor waiter Yes, sir. What would you like?

Guest We'd like to start with fruit juice, orange for me and grapefruit for my wife. Fresh juice, please. Not canned or frozen.

Floor waiter Right, sir. One fresh orange and one fresh grapefruit.

Guest Good. And then bacon, egg, and tomato for me and two soft-boiled eggs for my wife. And toast, butter, and marmalade. Do you have different marmalades?

Floor waiter Yes, sir. We'll put a selection of preserves on your tray. And is it tea or coffee?

Guest Tea, please, but with lemon, not milk.

Floor waiter Very good. And when is it for?

Guest Oh, about 7.30 would be fine.

Floor waiter Fine, and could you give me your name, sir?

Guest It's Sands. Mr and Mrs Sands, room 226.

Floor waiter Thank you, sir.

Dialogue 2

First guest That air-conditioning system sure makes a difference, doesn't it? It's really cool in here. Now what will you have, Beth? How about a whisky before we have lunch?

Second guest Oh no. Not for me; not in the middle of the day. But I'd love a long drink, a Campari, say, with lots of ice and soda water.

First guest That's a good idea. Why don't you have a Campari and soda, too, Muriel?

Third guest No, I'd rather have a beer. A bottle of cold lager is what I need. It's so hot out there. I feel I've been in an oven all morning.

First guest OK, barman; a Campari with plenty of ice and soda, a cold bottle of lager, a Scotch on the rocks for me and, George, what about you?

Fourth guest A glass of dry white wine, Stewart. Well-chilled.

First guest OK, barman. Have you got all that?

Barman Yes, sir. I have.

First guest Good. Put it on my bill, would you? The name's Stewart Carter. Room 714. Here's my Key Card.

Barman Thank you, Mr Carter.

Dialogue 3

Waiter Good morning, Mrs Taylor. Lovely day, isn't it?

Guest It certainly is. We're planning to go up into the mountains this afternoon.

Waiter Good idea. You'll have a wonderful view today.

Guest But before we go we'd like a snack.

Waiter Certainly. What can I get you?

Guest A ham sandwich and a coffee for me, and my husband would like a pâté sandwich and a shandy.

Waiter Shandy – that's half beer and half lemonade, isn't it?

Guest That's right. It's just the thing in this sort of weather.

Waiter And how would you like your coffee? Black or white?

Guest Oh, I prefer white, please. Those little espresso coffees that you serve are so strong.

Waiter So that's un sandwich jambon, un sandwich pâté, un café au lait et un panaché. Good. Why don't you visit Grasse while you're in the mountains? It's the centre of the perfume industry. I'm sure you'd find it interesting.

Guest That sounds a good idea. We'll do that, if we have time.

Waiter It's room 302, isn't it?

Guest Yes, that's right. Here's my Key Card.

Speaking
Making suggestions

Study the following examples.

Guest I'm looking for a good restaurant.   (The Concorde)
Hall porter *Why don't you try the Concorde?*

Guest I want to go to the British Airways office.   (a taxi)
Hall porter *Why don't you take a taxi?*

Now do the exercise on the tape, making the Hall Porter's suggestions in a similar way. After you speak, you will hear the Hall Porter's words on the tape.

Activities

There are many different ways of preparing and cooking food. Take mushrooms, for example. They can be (a) fried – fried mushrooms, (c) grilled – grilled mushrooms, or (f) deep-fried – deep-fried mushrooms. Now use the illustration below to decide how the various foods can be prepared and write out the descriptions.

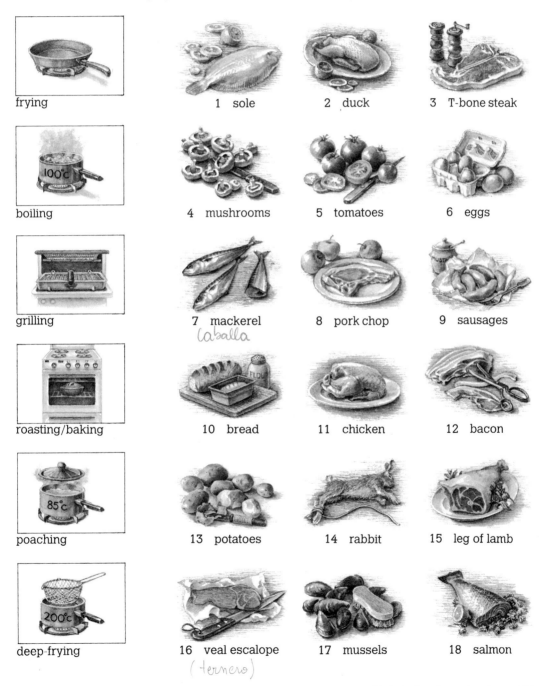

frying

boiling

grilling

roasting/baking

poaching

deep-frying

1 sole	2 duck	3 T-bone steak
4 mushrooms	5 tomatoes	6 eggs
7 mackerel *Caballa*	8 pork chop	9 sausages
10 bread	11 chicken	12 bacon
13 potatoes	14 rabbit	15 leg of lamb
16 veal escalope *(ternero)*	17 mussels	18 salmon

Listed below are the duties of a reception waiter, station waiter, and wine waiter in a restaurant. Decide in which order these activities should take place for the correct service of guests.

1 The station waiter brings the guests' first course.
2 The reception waiter checks on the time of the booking and the number of guests.
3 The wine waiter offers the guests the wine list and takes orders for apéritifs.
4 The wine waiter takes the order for wine.
5 The station waiter takes the order for food.
6 The reception waiter receives and welcomes the guests.
7 The wine waiter brings the wine.
8 The station waiter seats the guests.
9 The reception waiter takes the guests to their table.
10 The station waiter offers the guests the menus.
11 The wine waiter brings the apéritifs to the guests.

Writing

Writing A

Notice how the following pairs of sentences are combined using relative pronouns.

Examples:

Mr Torsen is the reservations clerk. He deals with the allocation of rooms. **(who)**
▶ Mr Torsen is the reservations clerk **who** deals with the allocation of rooms.

For each restaurant, the Good Eating Guide shows three speciality dishes. These speciality dishes are usually served à la carte. **(which)**
▶ For each restaurant, the Good Eating Guide shows three speciality dishes **which** are usually served à la carte.

Three stars are given to excellent restaurants. Only the very best food is available in these restaurants. **(where)**
▶ Three stars are given to excellent restaurants **where** only the very best food is available.

Combine the following pairs of sentences in a similar way, taking care to make any changes where they are necessary.

1 As requested, we have booked you two double rooms. These rooms look over the park. (which)
2 Here is our service list. The list gives details of the services available at the hotel. (that)
3 You can buy cigarettes and sweets at the hotel tobacconist. This is situated in the hotel lobby. (which)
4 Mr Franks is one of the duty managers. The duty managers deal with day to day problems. (who)
5 There are free shoe cleaning machines available. These can be found on the 2nd and 5th floors. (which)

6 We have received a telephone booking from European Mines. The company will confirm the booking by telex. (who)
7 The porter has gone to the chemist for the prescription. The porter will bring the prescription to your room. (which)
8 The Café Tour specializes in salmon. Salmon dishes are served by the Café Tour only in season. (which)
9 There is a car park adjoining the hotel. Only hotel guests may leave their cars in this car park. (where)
10 The hotel has a coffee shop on the ground floor. Beverages and snacks are served in the coffee shop all day. (where)

Writing B

Now write out the following passage, combining pairs of sentences where possible with **who, which**, and **where**.

The Hotel Simon has two restaurants. These restaurants are situated on the ground floor and the first floor of the hotel. The first-floor restaurant is called the Grill. The Grill has only an à la carte menu. The other restaurant is called the Simon. A set menu is usually served in this restaurant.

Monsieur Noiret is the reception head waiter. He deals with table reservations in the Grill and the Simon. Both these restaurants are very popular. The Grill is particularly busy in the evening, and so it is always necessary to reserve a table well in advance. In fact, the Grill is an excellent restaurant. First-rate cuisine and good wines are always available there.

Word study

à la carte p. 44, type of menu where each dish is individually priced.

air-conditioning system p. 50, system controlling air quality and temperature.

apéritif p. 47, alcoholic drink taken before a meal.

basic charges p. 44, charges that do not include any extra services or orders.

beverage p. 44, drink.

canned p. 49

a can of juice

chilled p. 50, made cold.

classification p. 44, way of dividing. *v* **classify.**

courses p. 44, different parts of a meal.

cuisine p. 44, cooking.

current p. 44, in use at the moment.

dessert p. 44, final course in a meal where something sweet is served.

entrée p. 44, course before the main course.

establishments p. 44, places of business.

herbs p. 47, plants whose leaves are used in cooking.

hors d'oeuvres p. 44, small dishes served at the beginning of a meal.

house speciality p. 44, special dish prepared by a restaurant.

indicated p. 44, shown. *n* **indication.**

in season p. 44, at certain times of the year.

main dish p. 44, most important or principal dish.

marmalade p. 49, type of jam made with oranges, lemons, etc.

overcharged p. 44, charged too much.

particularly p. 44, specially.

plain p. 44, simple.

preserves p. 49, marmalades and jams.

quality p. 44, level or degree of excellence.

reasonable p. 44, not too much.

recommend p. 44, speak well of. *n* **recommendation.**

Scotch on the rocks p. 50, Scotch whisky served with ice.

set meals p. 44, meals with a limited choice of dishes.

snack p. 50, light meal such as a sandwich.

soft-boiled eggs p. 49, eggs boiled for about three minutes.

... suits me p. 47, is to my liking.

VAT p. 44, Value Added Tax. A tax on goods and services in Britain.

wine list p. 47, list of wines served with a meal.

Revision Unit 1

The exercises in this unit are revision of some of the work studied in Units 1–4 of the course.

1 Asking questions

Example:

Find out   when he's leaving for London.
► When is he leaving for London?

Now make questions in a similar way.

Find out   1 how long Mr Wright wants to stay.
            2 when Mrs Sloane checked out.
            3 if they'd rather have white wine.
            4 which room the Lepics are staying in.
            5 if the manager was responsible.
            6 who the Browns should write to.
            7 how many non-stop London flights a day there are.
            8 when she is leaving the hotel.
            9 when the Golden Ball restaurant closes.
           10 what they'd like for dessert.

2 Vocabulary

Choose the correct word from those in the brackets in order to complete the following sentences.

1 The receptionist should give a (bill/receipt/confirmation) to a guest when valuables are deposited.
2 Dial 9 for an (extension/external/outer) line.
3 Payment may be made in any major European (cash/money/currency).
4 Guests should fill (in/up/of) a registration form.
5 Room 712 is (vacant/empty/not used) between 5th and 17th May.
6 Could you put me through (to/for/up) Mr Spencer in room 78, please.
7 A (payment/deposit/voucher) is required to confirm the booking.
8 Which (dessert/entrée/main dish) would you like before your steak?

3 Comprehension

Study the chart below and then answer the questions that follow.

FROM	LINE	TO	Till April 1	Till August 31
NEWCASTLE	Fred. Olsen-Bergen Line	BERGEN	No Service	£240.00
	DFDS/Tor Line	GOTHENBURG	No Service	£156.00
	DFDS	ESBJERG	£84.00	£120.00
	DFDS	OSLO	No Service	£150.00
HULL	North Sea Ferries	ROTTERDAM	£126.60	£177.00
	North Sea Ferries	ZEEBRUGGE	£118.20	£164.40
GT YARMOUTH	Norfolk Line	SCHEVENINGEN	£84.00	£103.50
FELIXSTOWE	Tor Line	GOTHENBURG	£120.00	£165.00
	Townsend Thoresen	ZEEBRUGGE	£29.50	£70.00
HARWICH	Prins Ferries	HAMBURG	£181.00	£201.50
	Prins Ferries	BREMERHAVEN	£169.50	£187.50
	Fred. Olsen-Bergen	KRISTIANSAND	No Service	£240.00
	DFDS	ESBJERG	£84.00	£120.00
	Sealink	HOOK OF HOLLAND	£56.00	£77.00
SHEERNESS	Olau Line	VLISSINGEN	£54.00	£57.00
DOVER	Sealink	OSTEND	£40.00	£42.00
	Sealink	DUNKIRK	£40.00	£42.00
	Sealink	CALAIS	£40.00	£42.00
	Seaspeed	CALAIS	£40.80	£60.00
	Townsend Thoreson	CALAIS	£26.50	£42.00
	Sealink	BOULOGNE	£40.00	£42.00
	Seaspeed	BOULOGNE	£40.80	£70.00
	Townsend Thoreson	ZEEBRUGGE	£26.50	£55.00
FOLKESTONE	Sealink	OSTEND	£40.00	£42.00
	Sealink	BOULOGNE	£40.00	£42.00
	Sealink	CALAIS	£40.00	£42.00

Cheapest crossing from England – A family of four in a Ford Cortina

1 What is the cheapest way to travel to Boulogne off-season?
2 How many companies operate ships to Calais?
3 What is the difference between the off-season and the high-season price for travellers going from Folkestone to Calais using Sealink?
4 In season, is Folkestone–Ostend as expensive as Dover–Ostend?
5 Which companies serve Zeebrugge, and from which ports?
6 How do you get to Gothenburg in March?

4 Verb tenses and forms

In the following sentences, place the word(s) in brackets in the correct tense and/or form.

1 At the moment, the tourist industry ... very quickly. (grow)
2 The London flight ... at 18.00 daily. (leave)
3 Mr Thomas ... yesterday morning at 9.00. (check in)
4 Mr Smith ... to order his meal. (still wait)
5 Fruit juices ... before they are served. (should chill)
6 Normally, the Hotel International ... individual bookings in writing. (not confirm)
7 The bookings ... ten days ago. (confirm)
8 I ... a menu yet. (not look at)
9 If Mr Shaw ..., I'll give him your message. (ring)
10 Traveller's cheques ... at the cash desk. (can change)

5 Multiple choice

Complete the following sentences in the correct way.

1 The main purpose of the key card is to show

   a. that a guest has confirmed his reservation.
   b. that a guest has paid a deposit.
   c. to the head waiter for a table reservation.
   d. services, facilities, tariff, and room number.

2 A room status system does not show

   a. the number of rooms available in any one day.
   b. the length of stay of an arrival.
   c. the room number allocated to arrivals.
   d. the number of people expected.

3 The most convenient way of registering a large group is

   a. a registration book.
   b. individual forms.
   c. a special room list.

4 If a guest wants to cash a personal cheque, the receptionist should

   a. ask the guest to sign it on the back.
   b. refuse to do it.
   c. check with the duty manager.
   d. always change it.

5 VAT is

   a. a service charge.
   b. a type of bill.
   c. an extra charge.
   d. a tax on service provided.

6 After greeting a new guest the receptionist's first action should be to

   a. check the guest's reservation.
   b. ask the guest the length of his stay.
   c. ask the guest to register.
   d. call the luggage porter.

7 A credit card is used primarily to

   a. obtain money when banks are closed.
   b. identify the writer of a cheque.
   c. purchase goods and services.

6 Translation

Translate the following words and expressions into your own language.

1 a. suburbs, b. off-season, c. fortnight, d. convenient

2 a. laundry, b. valuables, c. medical attention, d. personal cheque

3 a. frying, b. deep-frying, c. boiling, d. grilling

4 a. three course meal, b. dessert, c. wine list, d. set meal

5 a. grapefruit, b. grapes, c. banana, d. cucumber, e. melon, f. peas, g. celery, h. carrot, i. onion, j. garlic

6 a. roast lamb, b. boiled potatoes, c. grilled sole d. poached eggs, e. fried tomatoes, f. fresh lemon juice

7 Verbs and nouns

Complete the following table.

verb	noun	verb	noun
1 confirm	confirmation	9	cancellation
2 reserve	......	10 select	......
3 book	......	11 allocate	......
4	identification	12 sign	......
5 enquire	......	13	cash
6 alter	......	14	recommendation
7	clarification	15 charge	......
8 telex	......	16 register	......

8 Letter writing

Write replies to the following letters agreeing to the requests.

1 From: Leonard Freeman, Apt. 7, 2092 Berkeley Way, San Francisco, California 94010, USA.
Request: Double room from 7.6.82 for 4 nights. View over park.

2 From: Mrs Dobson, 46A Linfield Avenue, London N.W.2.
Request: 2 adjoining singles with bath from 21.7.82 for a fortnight.

3 From: Danielle Massoni, 11 Avenue Lepic, Montpellier, France.
Request: Change her booking of one single from 18.8.82 for one night to two singles for the same period. Garage space also required.

9 Description

Answer the following questions.

1 When showing new guests to a room, what are the most important hotel facilities to show them?

2 List what information is requested from an overseas visitor in your country.

3 Describe three room status systems.

4 You are working in Advance Reservations when an unknown man phones you to make a booking for later that afternoon which you are able to accept. List (1) the information you should obtain from him and (2) the information you should give him.

10 Job descriptions

Complete the following organization chart using the list of job titles below.

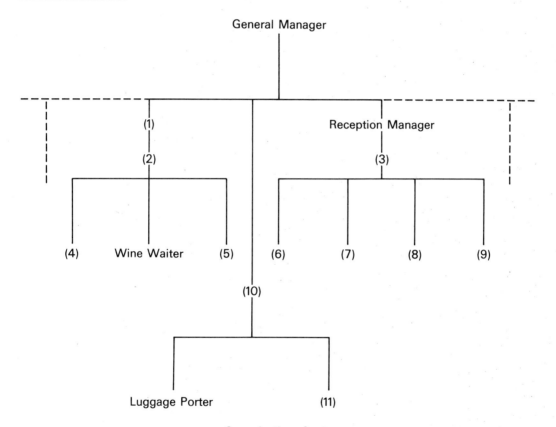

Organization chart

Cashier	Receptionist
Night Porter	Head Porter
Head Waiter	Reception Waiter
Advance Reservations Clerk	Enquiry Clerk
Station Waiter	Head Receptionist
Restaurant Manager	

Unit 5
Food service 2

Reading and Listening

Reading

The range of food service found in hotels and restaurants today is extensive. In the first category, there are restaurants offering the highest grade of service with a full à la carte menu. This includes dishes served by the waiter from a trolley in the dining room, and is known as gueridon service. The gueridon waiter must always be skilled, for he has to carry out procedures such as filleting, carving, and cooking speciality dishes at the table.

↙ cut the
meat

1 napkin /serviette
2 soup spoon
3 fish knife and fork
4 joint knife and fork
5 dessert spoon and fork

6 sideplate
7 side knife
8 wine glass
9 ashtray
10 salt, pepper

A second, less complicated, type of service is silver service where the menu can be either à la carte or table d'hôte. In this system, the food is prepared in the kitchen and then put on to silver flats and presented to the guests in the dining room. A third form of table service, used mainly with a table d'hôte menu, is plate service. Here, the waiter receives the meal already plated from the service hotplate and only has to place it in front of the guest and make sure that the correct cover is laid and the necessary accompaniments are on the table. Plate service is often offered where there is a rapid turnover and speedy service is necessary. It also demands less equipment for the service of the meal and is, therefore, labour-saving in such tasks as washing-up. In a fourth type of service, called self-service, a customer collects a tray from the service counter, chooses his dishes and selects the appropriate cutlery for the meal.

Today, with ever-increasing needs for economy, many establishments usually prefer a variety of types of service. Tourist hotels, for example, frequently offer a combination of self-service and plate service for breakfast and another combination of self-service and silver service for luncheon.

Reading check

1 What kinds of skills does a waiter require for gueridon service?
2 Why is plate service labour-saving?
3 What kinds of service are used with a table d'hôte menu?
4 What is the difference between silver service and plate service?
5 Why is self-service often used by hotels?

Listening

Mr and Mrs Drayton have entered the Restaurant Djebel, a family restaurant in the centre of Tunis. On the cassette, you will hear them order lunch.

Waiter Bonjour Madame. Bonjour Monsieur.

Mrs Drayton Bonjour. Have you a table for two, please?

Waiter Certainly. Where would you like to sit? By the window or further back?

Mrs Drayton I think we'd prefer by the window so that we can watch the people in the street.

Waiter Right. Won't you sit down?

Mr Drayton Thank you very much. This is pleasant.

Waiter Yes, it's a beautiful day today. What would you like to order?

Mrs Drayton Do you think you could explain the menu to us? You see, our French isn't good enough and we don't speak any Arabic at all.

Waiter Of course. We serve a fixed price three course lunch at 3 dinars 500 millimes and you can make your choice for each course.

Mr Drayton What's for starters?

Waiter There's brik à l'oeuf, that's tuna fish and an egg deep-fried in a pastry case, mechouia, a salad made with grilled tomatoes and peppers, or vegetable soup. Which would you prefer?

Mr Drayton I think I'll have the soup.

Mrs Drayton I'd rather have the brik à l'oeuf. It sounds very good.

Waiter Right. And for the main course, there's couscous, chicken, or steak.

Mr Drayton Well, couscous is a bit spicy for me. I think I'll have the steak.

Mrs Drayton Steak for me, too, please.

Waiter How would you like them cooked?

Mrs Drayton I don't like my steaks too underdone. Make mine well done.

Mr Drayton Rare for me, please.

Waiter Fine. What would you like to go with your steaks?

Mrs Drayton Chips and a green salad, please.

Mr Drayton I'll have chips. And peas, if you have them.

Waiter Yes, that's fine. And what would you like to drink? Bottled beer? Wine?

Mrs Drayton We like wine better.

Waiter We have a very pleasant house wine served by the carafe.

Mr Drayton Yes. I think a carafe of red would do nicely.

Mrs Drayton It isn't too dry, is it?

Waiter No, no. It's a medium wine.

Mrs Drayton Good. We'll have that then. And also a bottle of mineral water.

Listening check

1 Why does Mrs Drayton prefer to sit by the window?
2 What does the set meal consist of?
3 Why does Mrs Drayton ask the waiter to explain the menu?
4 What does Mr Drayton order for his first two courses?
5 How do the Draytons want their steaks cooked?
6 What kind of red wine doesn't Mrs Drayton like?

Language study

Study the following table.

	Mrs Sobell	Mr Sobell
1 red or white wine	red	white
2 dry wine or sweet wine	sweet	dry
3 steak or chicken	steak	chicken
4 sit inside or outside	outside	inside
5 pay by cash or by credit card	cash	credit card
6 order now or later	now	later
7 the table d'hôte menu or à la carte	à la carte	table d'hôte
8 coffee at the table or in the lounge	table	lounge

Notice how we can talk about the things we prefer in different ways.

Example:

Do you prefer red wine or white wine?
▶ I prefer red wine but Mr Sobell prefers white.

Would you rather have sweet wine or dry wine?
▶ I'd rather have sweet wine but Mr Sobell would rather have dry.

Now make similar questions and answers for 3–8 on the table.

Degree

Examples:

Is your steak rare **enough**?
▶ I'm afraid it's **too** rare. I can't eat it.

Is your steak **too** well done?
▶ No, it's not well done **enough.** I like it **very** well done.

In a similar way, answer the following questions.

1 Is your wine too dry?   No, ... I like ....
2 Is your couscous spicy enough?   I'm afraid .... I can't ....
3 Are we early enough for dinner?   I'm afraid .... You will ....
4 Is the six o'clock flight too early?   No, ... I must ....
5 Is your coffee strong enough?   I'm afraid .... I can't ....
6 Is the Hotel Park big enough?   I'm afraid .... I can't ....
7 Is your martini too weak?   No, ... I like ....
8 Is your room warm enough?   I'm afraid .... I like ....

Word order

It is important in English that we pay special attention to the order of words in a sentence.

Examples:

The newspapers are delivered. (at nine o'clock, to Reception)
▶ The newspapers are delivered **to Reception at nine o'clock.**

Receptionists must deal with the guests' problems. (always, politely)
▶ Receptionists must **always** deal **politely** with the guests' problems.

The table below can help you to remember the correct order.

how often ⟶ how	⟶ where	⟶ when
always	politely	to Reception	at nine o'clock

Now place the words in brackets correctly in the following sentences.

1 An à la carte menu is available. (in the evening, always, in the Dar Marhaba restaurant)
2 They ate in the hotel restaurant. (very well, never)
3 The waiter laid the table. (badly, often)
4 Sixty rooms are reserved by Johnson Tours. (in August, in the Hotel Park)
5 The gueridon waiter carved the roast beef. (skilfully, always)
6 The Night Porter was on duty. (at ten o'clock, every evening)

Listening and Speaking

Mary Burton, a tour group leader, is discussing the eating arrangements for her tour party with Hassan Labidi, an Assistant-Manager at the Sousse Palace Hotel. While you are listening to their conversation, complete the table below.

meal times	1 Breakfast 2 Lunch 3 Dinner
special diets	4 5
contents of picnic lunch	6

Labidi Hello again, Mary. Was the journey over with the tour group all right?

Burton Fine. There weren't too many problems. Just the usual things to take care of.

Labidi Well, the weather looks very good, so I think you'll have a quiet week.

Burton I hope so. And how about you? Are you busy?

Labidi Very. The hotel is nearly full. This has meant a slight change in the times of meals.

Burton Ah. Let me have them now.

Labidi It's mainly the dinner arrangements. We haven't enough staff for everybody so there are two sittings, one from seven o'clock till half past eight and another from half past eight till ten.

Burton Which sitting are we?

Labidi The first.

Burton Good. I'm sure they'll prefer eating earlier. What about the times for lunch and breakfast?

Labidi Breakfast is at the same time as usual, eight o'clock until nine thirty, but we have altered the lunch time a little. We've made it a self-service meal and it's now rather longer, from twelve thirty till two o'clock.

Burton Right. I've got that. I'll make sure that my party know what time they're supposed to eat.

Labidi Thank you, Mary. That would be a great help.

Burton There is another thing, too. A few members of the group will need special diets.

Labidi What exactly?

Burton There are three vegetarians.

Labidi That's no problem at all. There are plenty of non-meat dishes on the self-service counter at breakfast and lunch. And for dinner there are a number of vegetarian alternatives provided.

Burton Good. And there's one diabetic in the group: Mrs Lomax.

Labidi In her case, could you ask her to come and see me? I'll find out her exact requirements and make sure that the chef prepares a special menu for her.

Burton Thank you, Hassan. I think that's nearly everything I wanted to see you about.

Labidi What about day trips? Will you need any picnic lunches?

Burton Ah yes. I nearly forgot. We'll require a picnic lunch on Thursday. Are you providing a choice?

Labidi Yes, there's quite a wide choice of sandwiches and snacks. Then there's a selection of soft drinks and fruit. I'll give you the picnic lunch menu cards for your group and I would like them back on Tuesday. Perhaps you could put a note on the cards for the vegetarians and the diabetic.

Burton I'll do that. Well, thank you, Hassan. I think that really is everything now.

Labidi Good. I hope you have a pleasant week.

Burton So do I. But, as you say, if the weather continues like this I'm sure everyone will be content.

Labidi Right. Goodbye for now.

Burton Bye.

Speaking
Asking about preference

Study the following examples.

Guest I'll have a glass of wine, please. (red or white)
Waiter *Would you rather have red or white wine, sir?*

Guest Could we order our coffees now? (black or white)
Waiter *Would you rather have black coffee or white, sir?*

Now do the exercise on the tape, asking about the guests' preferences in a similar way.

When you have completed the exercise, listen to the instructions on the tape. You must repeat the exercise using the expression **would you prefer**.

Activities

Activity A

Look at the following list of dishes. They are taken from the two menus below. One is from an inexpensive self-service establishment and the other is from a one star restaurant. Decide which dish is from which menu and then arrange them in the correct order of presentation.

a.	Apple pie	h.	Sole Normande	o.	Grilled bacon and tomatoes
b.	Lasagne	i.	Vegetable soup	p.	Melon and Parma ham
c.	Hamburgers	j.	Vanilla ice cream	q.	Pork sausages and chips
d.	Pepper steak	k.	Shellfish cocktail	r.	Poached eggs Florentine
e.	Tomato juice	l.	Grilled mackerel	s.	Roast fillet of beef
f.	Lemon sorbet	m.	Crêpes Suzette	t.	Fried fish and chips
g.	Roast duck	n.	Grilled trout	u.	Salade de tomates

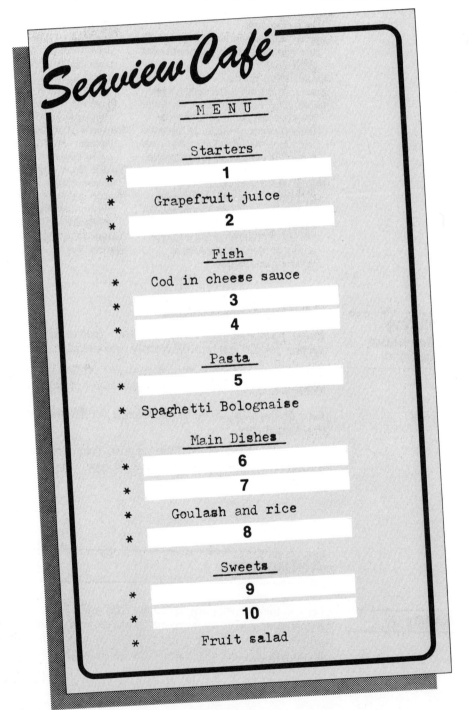

Seaview Café

MENU

Starters
* **1**
* Grapefruit juice
* **2**

Fish
* Cod in cheese sauce
* **3**
* **4**

Pasta
* **5**
* Spaghetti Bolognaise

Main Dishes
* **6**
* **7**
* Goulash and rice
* **8**

Sweets
* **9**
* **10**
* Fruit salad

Strand Restaurant

Table d'hôte menu 27.3.82

Hors d'oeuvres

Caviare	11
12	13

Poissons

14	Smoked salmon
	15

Oeufs

Eggs mayonnaise	16

Entrées

17	18
19	Lamb Pilau

Entremets

20	Pineapple with Kirsch
	21

Activity B

In the following chart, various foods and drinks are entered in the wrong box. For example, Tawny Port appears in Red Wine but it belongs in Dessert Wine. Re-arrange the chart so that the food and drinks appear in the correct boxes.

apéritifs	1 Rioja Chianti Sweet Vermouth	8 Hors d'oeuvres
sparkling wine	2 Burgundy Dry Vermouth Campari	9 Veal
white wine	3 _opporto_ Ruby Port Liqueur Brandy Hock _german white_ Riesling	10 Beef
rosé wine	4 Chablis Beaujolais	11 Coffee
red wine	5 Champagne Tawny Port Beaune	12 Chicken Dessert
dessert wine	6 Madeira Rosé d'Anjou Medium Sherry _Jerez_	13 Fish
liqueurs	7 Cointreau Dry Sherry	14 Lamb

Writing

The Catering Manager of the Grand Hotel du Sahara in Sfax has received a letter from a London football club which is planning a second tour of Tunisia. The club would like to reserve the Oasis Room for a dinner for 25 people on 17 June. Unfortunately this is not possible as the room is already booked on that date. This is the letter the Catering Manager sent to the club, in which he regrets that he is unable to accept the booking.

GRAND HOTEL DU SAHARA

Sfax · Tunisia

Mr N Brimble
Administrative Officer
West Queen's Park Football Club
London SE22

14.3.82

Dear Mr Brimble,

Thank you for your letter of 1 March 1982. I am very pleased to hear how much you enjoyed your previous visit to the Oasis Room and that you would like to visit us again. Unfortunately the Oasis Room is not available on the date you mention. It was reserved some time ago. It is available on 16 June but after that not until 21 June. If that is not convenient I can recommend the Sahel Suite at the Sfax Palace Hotel which is in the same chain as us.

Yours sincerely,

Mohammed Mansour

Mohammed Mansour
Catering Manager

Notice how Mr Mansour offers alternative arrangements, a different date in his own hotel or similar facilities in another hotel in the same chain.

Using Mr Mansour's letter as an example, now write letters regretting that you cannot accept the following requirements, but suggesting alternative arrangements, if possible. You are writing from the Advance Reservations Office of the hotel where Mr Mansour works. You should date your letters 29.3.82.

to	request	reply
1 Mr and Mrs B. Sharp Tremandan The Pass Manitoba Canada	double room with bath for 14 nights from 17.5.82	double without bath available, or double with bath in Hotel Belami, same chain and standard
2 Sebastian Grimes 61 Carr Precinct Ipswich, Suffolk England	single room with shower for 5 nights from 18.4.82	not possible at all because of large international convention in Sfax
3 M. Bernard Huppert Nylotex S.A. B.P. 892 Nevers France	wishes to extend his 7 day s/b booking (from 12.6.82) to 10 days	only s/sh available for the three day extension, or 10 days in s/b possible in Hotel Belami

Word study

accompaniments p. 61, equipment on a dining table such as salt, pepper, etc.
appropriate p. 61, suitable.
carafe p. 62, open glass container for wine, water, etc.
carving p. 60, cutting meat, etc.
category p. 60, type; class.
chips p. 62, deep-fried fingers of potato; French fries (US); pommes frites (Fr).
consist of p. 62, is composed of; is made of.
couscous p. 62, a North African dish consisting of meat and vegetables in a spicy sauce, served with semolina.
cover p. 61, the equipment on a dining table laid for each customer.
cutlery p. 61, knives, forks, spoons, etc.
diabetic p. 65, a person with the disease **diabetes** which makes it necessary to limit the amount of sugar eaten.
diets p. 65, restricted eating programmes. *v* **diet**.
economy p. 61, saving money. *v* **economize**.
extensive p. 60, wide.

filleting p. 60, removing the bones from fish, meat, etc.

flats p. 61, large serving plates.

grade p. 60, level.

house wine p. 62, restaurant's own wine.

labour-saving p. 61, work limiting.

mineral water p. 62, natural water sold in bottles.

previous p. 69, last.

procedures p. 60, methods; ways of doing things.

rare p. 62, only cooked a little; underdone.

sittings p. 64, services of a meal.

skilled p. 60, good at his work. *adj* **skilful**.

soft drinks p. 65, non-alcoholic cold drinks.

spicy p. 62, strong tasting because of high pepper or chili content.

table d'hôte p. 61, restricted choice.

tasks p. 61, jobs.

turnover p. 61, number of customers arriving and leaving.

vegetarians p. 65, people who don't eat meat and other animal products.

washing-up p. 61, cleaning the plates, cutlery, etc.

well done p. 62, well cooked.

Unit 6
Local tours

Reading and Listening

Reading

Here is a description of a Spanish resort taken from a Letts Holiday Guide.

Estartit

This popular summer resort has one of the finest sand beaches of the Costa Brava — the Playa de Pals. Formerly a little fishing port, where the inhabitants fished for sardine and anchovy, it has, in a few years, achieved international status without losing its appeal.

Just off the coast lie a group of four islands known as the Medas Isles and a little farther north is the Foadada Rock. Inhabited in Roman times, these islands later became deserted. Now you can take boat trips to them to swim, fish or simply sunbathe.

There is little to see in Estartit itself. In fact, it is hardly more than a main street — Calle Sante Ana — which runs parallel to the sea and contains some good boutiques and small souvenir shops. If you want to shop, the best day to visit Estartit is on Thursday, which is market day.

For a small resort, Estartit has plenty of night life. For first-class evening entertainment, often with an international floor show, it is worth climbing the hill to the Club El Catalan, and, in the village itself, the Galeon usually has a floor show, with dancing to recorded music. Young people usually go to the St. Tropez discotheque.

Anyone wishing to travel from Estartit to Torella de Montgri will be able to take the bus, which leaves at two-hourly intervals from Estartit.

· · · · · ·

1 sightseeing coach
2 news-stand
3 kiosk
4 telephone box
5 pavement café

1 Where is the Foadada Rock situated?
2 What activities can be carried out in the Medas Isles?
3 What does the Calle Sante Ana have to offer the tourist?
4 Why is Thursday the best day for shopping in Estartit?
5 Which three establishments are suggested for night-time entertainment?

Listening

Mr and Mrs Hill are in Spain for the first time. Listen to their conversation with Miss Lorca in one of the Tourist Information Offices in Barcelona.

Lorca Good morning. Can I help you?

Mr Hill Yes. We're staying in Barcelona for a few days and then we're visiting Madrid. Could you give us some advice about things to do here?

Lorca With pleasure. Let me tell you some of the things to do and then I'll give you some brochures and recommend some guide books as well.

Mr Hill Thank you.

Lorca You'd like to go sightseeing first, I expect. Why not have a walk down Las Ramblas before you do anything else? You'll get the atmosphere of the town there. There are pavement cafés where you can sit and watch the world go by, kiosks selling souvenirs, news-stands where you can get British and American newspapers and magazines, and a great number of good shops, bars, and restaurants.

Mrs Hill Yes, they mentioned the Ramblas at the hotel.

Lorca If you go to the end of the Ramblas, there's a square with a column that commemorates Christopher Columbus. You can climb up inside the monument and get a wonderful view over the port and the city.

Mrs Hill What's that big hill on the right as you look towards the harbour?

Lorca That's the Mountain of Montjuich.

Mrs Hill I see. Where is the most interesting architecture?

Lorca Have a look at Gaudi's Church of the Holy Family. It's world famous. The buildings in the old quarter are very interesting, too. Most of them date back to medieval times.

Mr Hill What about other amenities?

Lorca Oh, there are very good museums, art galleries, concert halls and so on. Ah, excuse me, I'll have to answer that. Why don't you take a guided tour? It's the best way of getting to know the city and it's not at all expensive.

Mrs Hill That's a good idea. Where do we go for that?

Lorca The next bus leaves from this office in a quarter of an hour.

Mr Hill Fine.

Lorca Here's an entertainment guide with details of events in Barcelona this week. The brochures are on those shelves. Help yourselves.

Mr Hill Right. Thank you for your help.

Lorca Not at all. Goodbye.

1 Where are Mr and Mrs Hill going when they leave Barcelona?
2 Where did the Hills first hear about Las Ramblas?
3 Where can you get a good view of Barcelona?
4 When does the next tour bus leave?
5 Where are the brochures?

Language study

Using prepositions

Notice how the prepositions are used below to describe position and direction.

Just **off** the coast lies a group of islands.
You can take boat trips **to** the Medas Isles.
There is a discotheque **in** the village.

Now study the following table and choose the correct prepositions from the table to complete the sentences below.

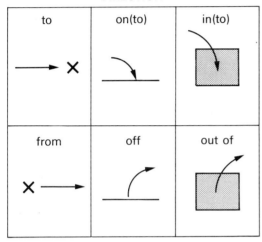

DIRECTION

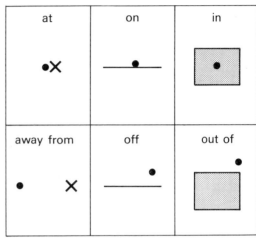

POSITION

1 The tour buses depart ⟨from⟩ .. the central square at two-hourly intervals.
2 There are many interesting buildings ⟨in⟩ the old quarter of the city.
3 The medieval monastery is situated seven miles ⟨from⟩ the town.
4 I'll wait for you ⟨at⟩ the reception desk.
5 They travelled ⟨from⟩ Madrid to Barcelona overnight.
6 The coach driver drove ⟨away from⟩ the main road in order to visit the craft centre near Cordoba.
7 I would like a table ⟨away from⟩ the window. It's too bright today.
8 You can find the Hotel Jorge just ⟨off⟩ the Ramblas. (saliendo)
9 One moment, I've left my wallet ⟨on⟩ the table.
10 His room looked ⟨onto⟩ the main street.

Future time

Notice how we can use the Simple Present and the Present Continuous to talk about the future.

The next boat train for London **leaves** at six o'clock.
Mrs Francis **is meeting** her friends at the Akropolis tomorrow.

The Simple Present is used to refer to future events that are part of a fixed timetable or programme. The Present Continuous is used to refer to an individual arrangement or plan for the future.

In the following sentences, place the verb in brackets in either the Simple Present or the Present Continuous.

1 I ... to the cinema tomorrow afternoon. (go)
2 The chef ... a special dinner for the managing director and his wife next Friday. (prepare)
3 The guided tour ... from the Information Office at ten o'clock this evening. (depart)
4 We ... two weeks in Paris this August. (spend)
5 The first performance at the theatre ... at 17.30 tonight. (begin)
6 Mrs Sloane ... her sister for lunch at 13.00 tomorrow. (meet)

Abbreviations

Match each of the following abbreviations with the full form that it stands for in the list given below. Then learn them.

1 kgs	9 no.	17 pm
2 A.C.	10 oz	18 hrs
3 PO	11 sae	19 Ave
4 lbs	12 am	20 Rd
5 tel.	13 h & c	21 fr
6 km	14 °F	22 arr
7 dep	15 St	23 v
8 °C	16 incl.	24 eg.

before midday a. m   kilograms   number
volts   telephone   ounces
hot and cold 13   francs   Avenue
after midday   inclusive   hours
degrees Centigrade   pounds   Road
air conditioning   Street   arrival
stamped addressed envelope kilometre   for example
degrees Fahrenheit   Post Office   departure

Listening and Speaking

Listening

While you are listening to the guide on a tourist boat on a sightseeing trip in central Stockholm, look at the map of the city. It shows you the route the boat follows and all the places the guide mentions during the trip. Choose a name from the list to identify each of the numbers on the map.

a Central Station   e The Lock   i Royal Palace
b German Church   f Museum of Modern Art   j Town Hall
c Grand Hotel   g Oldest House in Stockholm
d National Museum   h Former Parliament Building

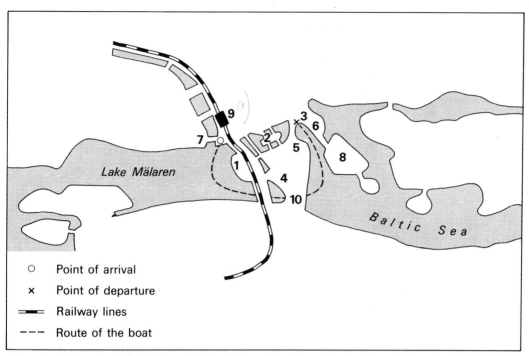

Sightseeing boat trip round the old city in Stockholm

Guide Good afternoon, ladies and gentlemen. My name is Gunilla Bergman and I welcome you on board this boat, the Sightseeing XII, which leaves shortly for a one hour trip round the Old City of Stockholm. Before we start I'd like to tell you about our route. The Old City is in fact a small island. It's not possible for us to go all the way round it because the water to the north of it moves too fast for boats to travel there. The reason for this fast movement is that the water to the east of the island is the Baltic Sea. To the west, the water is fresh, not salt. It is the beginning of Lake Mälaren. At this point the lake water flows rapidly into the sea. Our trip will end at a point close to the Central Railway Station. ... As you can see, we are now moving away from the land. The building almost next to us on the left is the Grand Hotel and beyond that you can see the National Museum which contains older art. If you walk past that museum, over the bridge and on to the island Skeppsholmen, you can visit the Museum of Modern Art, which has more recent works.

If you look over to the right now, you can't miss the Royal Palace. It has more than one room for every day of the year. ... We are now going to leave the Baltic Sea, ladies and gentlemen, by going through Slussen, the Lock. In it, we'll be lifted up to the level of the lake water. ... Right, now we are on Lake Mälaren. The bridge that we're now passing under carries the railway lines to the south and the west of Sweden. If you look over to the right now, you will be able to see the German Church. It's in the middle of the Old City and, as you can see, quite high up. ... We're now passing Helgeandsholmen, that small island on the right, next to the Old City. There you can find the oldest house in Stockholm. ... If you look over to the right now, you can see the former Parliament Building behind the railway and road bridges, and in front of you is the Town Hall. We go quite close to it before we tie up at our arrival point near the Central Station. Thank you for your attention, ladies and gentlemen, and I hope you have enjoyed the trip.

Speaking

Giving
information
about times

Study the following examples.

Tourist When does the London train leave?   (10.05)
Railway clerk *It leaves at five past ten.*

Tourist At what time does the performance begin?   (7.15)
Theatre clerk *It begins at quarter past seven.*

Now do the exercise on the tape, making replies
in a similar way and using the times given below.

Guest When does the next New York flight depart?
Receptionist (11.20)

Guest At what time does the restaurant close?
Receptionist (22.45)

Receptionist When does the night porter finish his duty?
Manager (7.30)

Receptionist When does Mrs Hales require her breakfast?
Manager (6.50)

Guest At what time does my bus leave?
Receptionist (3.35)

Activities

Activity A

In a recent survey of British holidaymakers visiting Italian resorts,
questions were asked about what facilities were considered the most
important for a holiday abroad. Here are the results of that survey.

facilities	Percentage (%) of holidaymakers who thought that this was:		
	very important	quite important	not important
1 Weather	78	12	10
2 Food	68	24	8
3 Comfort of hotel	45	52	3
4 Hotel services	42	56	12
5 Night life	31	30	39
6 Distance of hotel from beach	44	20	26
7 Distance of hotel from town	29	30	41
8 Sports	20	35	45
9 Shopping	32	44	24
10 Day-time entertainment	18	46	42
11 Amenities for children	15	13	72
12 Local tours to places of interest	23	34	42

1 Put all the facilities in the order of importance you think would
appeal to the following holidaymakers:
a. A husband and wife with three children under ten years old.
b. Two active young men aged 21 and 23.

2 Do you think the survey asked all the questions that were
necessary? If not, what other facilities are holidaymakers interested
in?

Activity B

Three tourists wish to make a half-day sightseeing trip round Paris.
They each have different requirements. There are no trips that will
make it possible for the tourists to stop everywhere and see
everything that they want. Compare their needs in the table and the
descriptions of the tours. Decide which of the tours best suits the
individual needs of each of the tourists.

tourist	would like to stop at	would like to see
Mr Shaw	Eiffel Tower Sacré Coeur Louvre	Opéra Champs Elysées Left Bank Arc de Triomphe
Mrs Ryan	Eiffel Tower Louvre Notre Dame Cathedral	Opéra Luxembourg Gardens Left Bank Sacré Coeur Panthéon
Miss Berg	Arc de Triomphe Sacré Coeur Notre Dame Cathedral	Opéra Left Bank Panthéon Montmartre

1 HISTORIC PARIS (frs. 95)
daily at 9.15 (3 hours)

Starting at the Opéra, this tour visits the
Marais, Place des Victoires, la Bastille,
and the Ile de la Cité in the heart of
Paris, with the Palais de Justice and
Conciergerie; then to the Left Bank,
passing the Boulevard St Michel and the
Sorbonne University. You will also see the
Panthéon. Stops are made at the Louvre
and the Luxembourg Gardens and there is
a detailed visit to Notre Dame Cathedral.

2 PARIS VISION (frs. 120)
daily at 10.00 (3 hours)

This is a wonderful tour; you travel in an ultra-
modern coach and a detailed commentary
is provided through individual earphones.
You see the Opéra, Montmartre, Sacré Coeur,
and then go down to the Place de la Concorde
and along the Champs Elysées to the Arc
de Triomphe, where a stop is made. Other
stops are made at Les Invalides and Notre
Dame. Return is via the Left Bank and the
Rue de Rivoli.

3 TUESDAY SPECIAL (frs. 110)
Tuesdays at 9.00 (3 hours)

A special tour of Paris guided in person by a Paris Travel Service Hostess. This tour includes stops at the Eiffel Tower and Montmartre with views over Paris from the steps of Sacré Coeur. You will see the Place de la Concorde, the impressive Champs Elysées, and the Arc de Triomphe.

4 MODERN PARIS (frs. 85)
daily at 13.45 (2½ hours)

This very interesting tour starts at the Opéra and passes the Madeleine, the Statue of Liberty, the Champs Elysées and the Place de la Concorde. Stops are made at the Arc de Triomphe and the Eiffel Tower and on the return part of the trip you will see the Champ de Mars.

Writing

Writing A

Study the town map below.

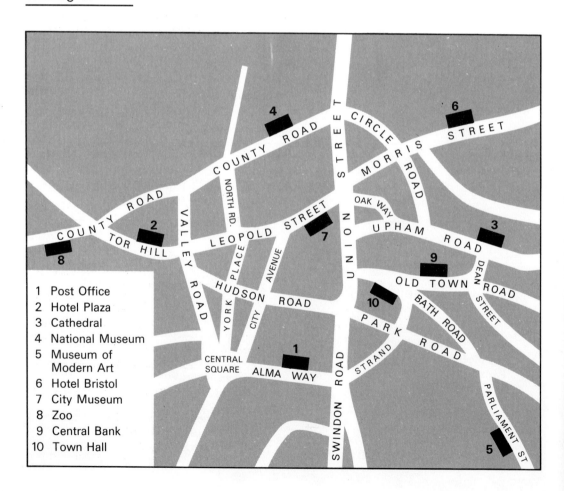

1 Post Office
2 Hotel Plaza
3 Cathedral
4 National Museum
5 Museum of Modern Art
6 Hotel Bristol
7 City Museum
8 Zoo
9 Central Bank
10 Town Hall

Notice how we can write out instructions for finding our way. How do you get from the Post Office to the City Museum? Turn right outside the Post Office and walk down Alma Way until you come to Central Square. Then turn right up City Avenue and continue as far as you can. Turn right into Leopold Street and you'll find the Post Office about half-way down on the right.

How do you get from the Post Office to the Museum of Modern Art? Turn left outside the Post Office and walk down Alma Way, across Swindon Road, into the Strand and then take the first right into Park Road. Continue down Park Road until Parliament Street, which is the first on the right. The Museum of Modern Art is a little way down on the right-hand side.

Writing B

Cover the instructions and try to write them out yourself.

Writing C

Now make instructions for the following routes.

1 How do you get from the Post Office to the Zoo?
2 What's the quickest way from the Cathedral to the National Museum?
3 What's the best route from the Hotel Plaza to the Central Bank?
4 How do you get from the Museum of Modern Art to the Hotel Plaza?
5 How do you get from the Hotel Plaza to the Cathedral?

Word study

abroad p. 78, in a foreign country; overseas.
amenities p. 74, places to go to and things to do.
appeal p. 73, attraction. *v* **appeal**.
architecture p. 74, buildings and styles of making them.
atmosphere p. 74, feeling; ambience.
boutiques p. 73, small shops.
brochures p. 74, small book or booklet giving information.
coast p. 73, the part of the land where it joins the sea.
column p. 74

commemorates p. 74, is in memory of.
deserted p. 73, empty; without people.
discotheque p. 73, dance club with modern music.
entertainment p. 73, amusement, show or performance. *v* **entertain**.
events p. 74, happenings.
floor show p. 73, performance in a club or restaurant.
guide p. 74, a book or person giving information about a place. *v* **guide**.
harbour p. 74, port.
help yourselves p. 74, take what you want.
holidaymakers p. 78, people who are on holiday.
inhabitants p. 73, people who live in a place. *v* **inhabit**.
magazines p. 74, publications, usually weekly or monthly.

market p. 73, a place where people meet to buy and sell.

medieval p. 74, from the Middle Ages, about 1300–1500.

monument p. 74, something that commemorates.

night life p. 73, evening and night entertainment.

old quarter p. 74, the oldest part of a town.

on board p. 77, on (used of ships and planes).

parallel p. 73

resort p. 73, place where tourism is the main business.

souvenir p. 73, object that brings back memories.

sunbathe p. 73, lie in the sun to get a brown skin.

survey p. 78, scientific enquiry.

two-hourly intervals p. 73, every two hours.

world famous p. 74, known all over the world.

These lines are parallel

Unit 7
Complaints

Reading and Listening

Reading

14 West Brompton Road
Wolverhampton
Warwickshire

21.9.82

The Manager
Starway Tours
121-123 City Road
London
W1Y 7HE

Dear Sir

I have recently returned from your Starway Five Nations Tour – ST 104/5. I am very upset by the standards and the organization of this tour and I have a number of comments about it that I would like to make.

In general, the food was extremely poor and the service was very slow. On a number of occasions we had to wait over an hour for our meals. In one hotel there was a problem of overbooking. After a long and tiring journey, we discovered that this hotel had no accommodation for us. We were transferred to another hotel on the outskirts of the city. In your advertisement, you stated that all the hotels were located in city centres.

There were also a number of travel delays during the tour, and on one occasion my luggage was left off the coach. I only got it back a day later.

Finally, I think your staff should have handled these problems in a better way. Some of them were rather rude when complaints were made.

I feel that your company should consider an appropriate refund because of the bad service that was provided.

Yours faithfully,

M. Stamp

Muriel Stamp (Mrs)

1 What was wrong with the food service? *service slow*
2 Why did Mrs Stamp complain about the hotel transfer? *they were sent to*
3 What happened to Mrs Stamp's luggage? *left off the coach.*
4 What complaint was made about the staff of the tour company? *unhelpful.*
5 Why does Mrs Stamp want some of her money returned? *bad service provided.*

Listen to the receptionist in the Hotel International dealing with complaints.

Dialogue 1

Bryant Hello, is that Reception?

Receptionist Yes, it is.

Bryant This is Miss Bryant in room 142. I checked in about ten minutes ago.

Receptionist Ah yes, Miss Bryant. How can I help you?

Bryant You can help me by getting my bathroom put right. It's in an absolutely terrible condition. When I tried the shower, no water came out at all.

Receptionist Oh dear, I am sorry to hear that. I'll have it fixed immediately.

Bryant And that's not all. There's no soap, towel or toilet paper.

Receptionist I apologize for this, Miss Bryant. We're rather short-staffed at present. Housekeeping should have checked your room. We'll attend to it as soon as possible. There's been a misunderstanding.

Bryant That's all right. The most important thing is to fix it as soon as possible.

Dialogue 2

Brewster Good evening. My name is Brewster. There's a booking in my name. A single room, three nights.

Receptionist I'm awfully sorry, Mr Brewster, but we've let the room to someone else and there are no others available.

Brewster What do you mean, you've let the room? I made the booking weeks ago.

Receptionist I know, sir, but you should have checked in before six this evening. It's nearly ten now. There's a six p.m. release on all our rooms. It was in the letter of confirmation.

Brewster That's very pleasant, isn't it? My plane was four hours late. And now you tell me that you've let my room.

Receptionist I'm terribly sorry, but that is the situation. Let me see if I can book you another room in a nearby hotel, and we'll arrange the transfer.

Brewster I think that's the least you can do. Well, all right, go ahead. I've got to sleep somewhere.

Receptionist Good. Please take a seat and I'll soon have something arranged for you.

1 What is wrong with Miss Bryant's bathroom?
2 What does Miss Bryant think is the most important thing to get done?
3 Why has Mr Brewster arrived late?
4 Why should Mr Brewster have known about the six p.m. release?
5 What does the receptionist offer to do for Mr Brewster?

Language study

Causes of complaint

Should have done

Look at this picture of a hotel bedroom.

1	bed	6	ashtray
2	sheets	7	tray
3	wardrobe	8	lamp
4	carpet	9	books
5	waste-paper basket	10	curtain

It is not surprising that the guest who was given this room complained.
The Housekeeping staff did not do a number of things that they **should
have done** before the guest saw the room.

Examples:

change
▶ They **should have changed** the sheets.

close
▶ They **should have closed** the wardrobe.

Now say what other things the Housekeeping staff **should have done.**

1 make	5 open
2 vacuum	6 remove
3 clean	7 pick up
4 empty	8 replace

Getting things done

Staff often need to say that some other person will perform a service that a customer requests. Notice how this is done.

Examples:

There isn't any instant coffee in my room. (send up)
▶ I'**ll have** some **sent up.**

The glasses are dirty. (change)
▶ I'**ll have** them **changed.**

In a similar way, say that you **will have** the following things **done.**

1 The TV doesn't work in room 713. (fix)
2 There aren't any towels in my room. (send up)
3 My shower still isn't right. (repair)
4 You said you'd get me that prescription. (deliver to your room)
5 Are you sure this bill is correct? (check)
6 I've left my luggage in the room. (bring down)

Adverbs of degree

We can use the following adverbs to make an adjective stronger or weaker.

The hotel is | extremely / very / rather / quite | busy. | STRONGER ↑

Notice how we use these adverbs only before adjectives.

Examples:

The tour group complained about the long walk to the beach. (extremely)
▶ The tour group complained about the **extremely** long walk to the beach.

He checked out because of the poor service in the hotel (rather).
▶ He checked out because of the **rather** poor service in the hotel.

In a similar way, choose one of the adverbs to place in each of the following sentences.

1 Mr Lyons thought the souvenirs were expensive.
2 It was hot on the beach yesterday afternoon.
3 Miss Rikard was late for the meeting with the tour company.
4 He was tired after the nine-hour flight from London.
5 Customers often complained about the high telephone charges.
6 Mrs Dill was annoyed about the traffic noises from the street.

Listening and Speaking

Listening

Three guests at the Hotel International are making complaints to staff members there. While you are listening to their conversations, complete the table below.

person making complaint	friendly or unfriendly?	details of complaint	action taken
1 Mrs Dupont	*unfriedly*	*valuables stolen*	Call duty manager
2 *Mr Smith*	*friendly*	a. *line cut off.* b. bad line	*get in toud with operator.*
3 *Mr Jones*	*un ll*	a. tough steak b. *wine*	a. *Change* b. *try another*

Dialogue 1

Receptionist Good morning, Mrs Dupont. Is everything all right?

Dupont No, it's not. Someone's stolen some of my valuables – two rings and a gold watch.

Receptionist I'm very sorry to hear that, madam. Where were they?

Dupont In my room. And the door was locked. It can only be one of your staff. I want my things back. And fast.

Receptionist Well, I can certainly understand that you're upset about losing them and we'll do all we can to help. If they really are missing, it's a matter for the police.

Dupont What do you mean, 'if they are missing'? I told you they were.

Receptionist Yes, madam, but first I'll have one of the Housekeeping staff look through your room in case they're still there. But I must say that we can't be held responsible. You should have deposited the valuables with Reception. It says so on the Key Card.

Dupont That's not good enough. I want to see the manager. Immediately.

Receptionist I'll be glad to call the duty manager for you, madam, but he'll certainly say the same. We have very clear instructions about valuables and we must follow them.

Dialogue 2

Receptionist Reception. Can I help you?

Smith Yes. This is Sebastian Smith in room 704. I've tried to ring my wife in London twice and both times I was cut off.

Receptionist Did you actually speak to your wife, Mr Smith?

Smith Yes, it was the same both times. We spoke for maybe twenty seconds and then the connection was broken. The line was terribly bad, too. I could hardly hear her.

Receptionist I'm sorry to hear that, Mr Smith. That certainly shouldn't have happened. Would you give me your wife's number and I'll get in touch with the operator? He'll tell us if the fault is in their equipment or in ours. I'll call you back as soon as I can.

Smith Good. Thank you very much.

Dialogue 3

Manager You asked to see me, Mr Jones?

Customer I certainly did. I'm not at all happy.

Manager Perhaps you could tell me what the problem is exactly?

Customer It's my steak.

Manager What's wrong with it, sir?

Customer It's tough. When I complained to your waiter, he didn't take any notice.

Manager I am extremely sorry, sir. I'm sure the waiter didn't mean to be rude. Perhaps he didn't understand you correctly. He should have changed it.

Customer Well, why didn't he?

Manager A misunderstanding, sir. I'll have the steak changed immediately.

Customer Good. That's better. A little service at last. And another thing. This wine. I think it's corked.

Manager Are you quite sure, sir? That claret has been very good.

Customer Here. Taste it yourself.

Manager ... No, sir. There doesn't seem to be anything wrong with it. Perhaps it's a little dry for your taste. I would recommend you to try the Beaujolais next time.

Customer Right. Well, perhaps I will.

Manager Is that all, sir?

Speaking
Getting things done

Study the following examples.

Guest My steak is extremely tough.   (change)
Manager *I'll **have it changed** straight away.*

Guest The windows in my room are very dirty.   (clean)
Receptionist *I'll **have them cleaned** straight away.*

Now do the exercise on the tape, telling guests you will get things done for them in a similar way.

Activities

Activity A

Read this passage from a training book for tourist industry staff.

When you are dealing with complaints, you should listen carefully; be polite; and, except when it is absolutely necessary, don't comment until the customer has finished. Then, make a short, clear apology. After that, you should repeat the complaint. This is to make sure that you have fully understood the problem and that there are no misunderstandings. When possible, you should also note down what the customer has said. Next, you should decide who will deal with the complaint. If it is not a serious one, you can deal with it yourself. You should explain to the customer the action you plan to take and tell him when it will be done. If you decide that a manager should handle the complaint, you should first inform him and then arrange a meeting between him and the customer.

Now use the information in the passage to help you to complete the flow chart on the next page.

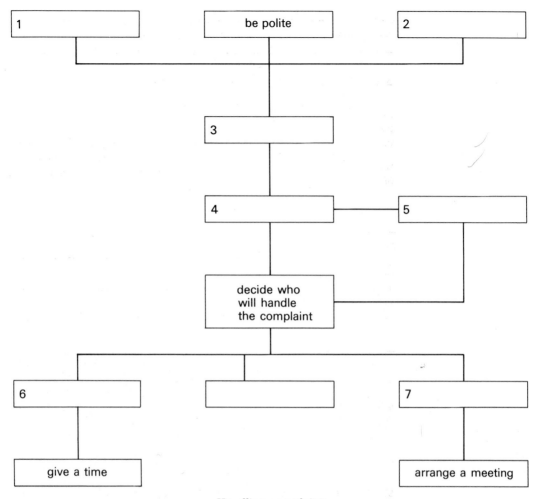

| 1 | | be polite | | 2 | |

| 3 |

| 4 | | 5 |

decide who
will handle
the complaint

| 6 | | | | 7 |

| give a time | | | | arrange a meeting |

Handling complaints

Activity B

Most businesses take complaints very seriously; but some complaints are more serious than others and some customers complain more than others. It is often the responsibility of an individual member of staff to deal with the problem. Sometimes, of course, it is necessary for the staff member to refer an unhappy customer to someone else, such as a manager.

Look at the following complaints that guests are making to staff at the Hotel International.

- Mrs Lyle says that she did not get her early morning call.
- Mr Lampard in room 702 is very annoyed about the loud music and voices from room 703.
- Miss Ainsty says there is no coffee in her room.
- Mr Shaw is complaining loudly in the restaurant about badly cooked meat.
- Mr Stein says his wallet is missing from his room.
- Mr Anderson is complaining about the air-conditioning for the fifth time in four days.

- Mrs Edwards says that she finds the floor waiter very rude.
- Mr Lean says that his bathroom shower doesn't work.
- Mr Fairfax is complaining in the lobby that the hotel has let his reserved room to someone else.
- Mrs White says she can never get an outside line.
- Mr Shepherd is not sure if the wine is corked.
- Mrs Parnell is most upset that her usual suite of rooms is not available.

Now decide which member of the hotel staff is best suited to deal with these complaints; perhaps the duty manager, the assistant manager, the head receptionist, a receptionist, a station waiter, the head waiter, or someone else. Give reasons for your choices.

Writing

Here is the main part of a letter of complaint to the Hotel International.

Dear Sir,

I must complain in writing about the service at the Hotel International last month. I stayed at the hotel for a fortnight, and this was my fifth visit.

There were a number of things wrong. First, the new self-service arrangement at lunch was not what I expected. Secondly, the service at dinner was very slow. Thirdly, the general standard of service in the hotel was very poor. The receptionists always seemed extremely busy; the hotel porter was never available; and I thought that the floor waiter was rather rude.

I do not usually complain but, as an old customer, I'm sure you will be interested in my comments.

Yours faithfully,

John Crewe

John Crewe

Here is the reply from the Manager of the Hotel International.

Dear Mr Crewe,

The Hotel International is always interested to hear the comments of its guests and we are glad that you have written to us.

I am extremely sorry that you found the service provided by Reception, the Hall Porter, and the Floor Waiter not up to our usual standard. I apologize for this and will make enquiries about it.

This year you took your holiday in August, which is our busiest month. The self-service arrangement for lunch is always used in July and August. However, I regret that you had slow service at dinner.

I hope we will continue to receive your custom and that, if you have a complaint, you will inform my staff immediately so that we can deal with the problem there and then.

Yours sincerely,

Alan Rey
Manager

Now write letters of reply to the following written complaints received by the Hotel International.

1 Mr Wainwright has complained about the standard of service in the Grill Restaurant. He says that he had to wait thirty minutes for his table, that the service was slow, and that the food was not very good.

2 Mrs Sherwood has complained that the hotel has not sent the hotel brochure and price list which she requested six weeks ago.

3 Mr Ambler has complained that his room was too small, that the people in the next room were noisy, and that the prices in the restaurant and bar were too high.

Word study

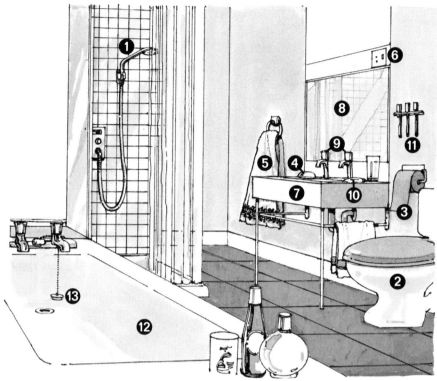

a bathroom

1 shower
2 toilet
3 toilet paper
4 soap
5 towel
6 razor socket
7 wash basin
8 mirror
9 taps
10 toothpaste
11 toothbrush
12 bath
13 plug

advertisement p. 84, notice of object or service for sale. *v* **advertise.**

apologize p. 85, am sorry. *n* **apology.**

attend to p. 85, deal with.

coach p. 84, comfortable bus, often used over long distances.

comments p. 84, things to say. *v* **comment.**

cork p. 89, stopper in top of wine bottle, etc.

corked p. 89, of low quality because of a poor **cork.**

cut off p. 88, unable to continue the call because of a broken connection.

delays p. 84, unscheduled periods of waiting.

discovered p. 84, found. *n* **discovery.**

fault p. 88, failure; breakdown.

fix p. 85, repair; put right; put in order.

handled p. 84, dealt with.

left off p. 84, not put on.

matter p. 88, subject; question.

missing p. 88, cannot be found.

nearby p. 85, close; near.

occasions p. 84, times.

outskirts p. 84, edge; limits.

overbooking p. 84, taking a number of bookings that is greater than the number of beds available. Another expression, for individual beds and rooms, is **double-booking.**

refund p. 84, repayment. *v* **refund.**

rude p. 84, not polite; impolite.

short-staffed p. 85, with fewer staff than necessary.

six p.m. release p. 85, not holding rooms after six p.m.

standards p. 84, levels of performance.

stated p. 84, said. *n* **statement.**

tough p. 88, hard and difficult to eat.

transferred p. 84, moved to. *n* **transfer.**

upset p. 84, angry and unhappy; annoyed. *v* **upset.**

Unit 8
Checking out

Reading and Listening

Reading

Every hotel needs to record the income it receives. Any system of recording charges should keep guests' bills up to date, identify the sales of different departments, and make financial control possible.

Twenty years ago, the tabular ledger was the most common method of recording charges in hotels, and is still used by some smaller establishments. However, since the introduction of cheaper billing machines, machine billing has replaced the 'tab' in many hotels. In larger establishments, a further development has been the use of the computer for handling accounts.

HOTEL OAXACA   Veracruz

```
    MRS    JARMAN/GODDARD        SUNSHINE REF: S22339/1
    DEPOSIT:    00.00


 Room    318           No of guests  3          Arrive  17/03/82
 Rate    2 000 pesos   Bill no   2601 283 W M 2   Depart  19/03/82


                       CHARGES      CREDITS              BALANCE

 17.03.82  Apartments     2 000                 233992
 18.03.82  Apartments     2 000                 (
 19.03.82  Ledger Transfer            4 000     S22339/1   00.00



 ACC. TO:       SUNSHINE HOLIDAYS
```

SERVICE AND TAX ARE   SIGNATURE _____
INCLUDED, GRATUITIES AT
YOUR DISCRETION   **PLEASE LEAVE YOUR KEY**

A computer bill

In computer billing, charges are entered into the computer by the bill office clerk using a keyboard terminal. No bill is produced until the guest is ready to settle his account. Then the cashier 'calls' the bill and it is printed out for the guest in a few seconds. If the hotel has wrongly charged a guest for an item, the cashier can make out an allowance slip.

ALLOWANCES			
Guest's Name		Arrival Date	
Authorized By		Departure Date	
Reason			
BREAKDOWN ON DEPARTMENTS		£	p
Room No.		TOTAL	

An allowance slip

The computer memory keeps a running total of every bill in the hotel. Control checks can be programmed into the computer. If a cashier does not post a charge correctly, it automatically queries the posting.

A financial statement is also automatically produced at the end of the day together with a full sales ledger which shows the total sales of each department and the totals for each room. A list of bills can also be produced for the credit control department.

When the computer has produced a bill for a guest, it is also able to handle the various methods of payment. If the guest pays in a foreign currency, the computer will use the current exchange rate and calculate the amount of change required. Credit card and ledger account details can be entered into the computer's memory. The cashier can then guarantee the credit status of any cards offered for payment.

All these facilities reduce the amount of paperwork and little time is spent waiting at the reception desk.

Reading check

1 What has replaced the 'tab' in many smaller hotels?
2 In which two ways does the computer memory help with payments?
3 In computer billing, when is a guest's bill printed out?
4 What is the purpose of programming control checks into the computer?
5 Why is it easier to check credit card payments in a computerized system?

Listening

A guest is leaving the Hotel Oaxaca, Veracruz. Listen to her conversation with the cashier.

Brown Good morning. I'd like to check out. The name's Brown, Sara Brown. Room 201.

Cashier Just a moment, Ms Brown, and I'll prepare your bill ... Here you are, then. That's the total amount payable at the bottom there.

Brown I can't believe it. I'm sure that's too much. Perhaps there's a mistake. Could you go through it with me?

Cashier Yes, of course. It's an itemized bill, as you can see. If there is a mistake, we'll soon discover it. A-P-T-S stands for Apartments. That's the basic room rate. You've been here since Sunday. That makes five nights and the Apartments charge is repeated five times. So that's OK. These charges here are for meals and drinks that you signed for.

Brown Yes. They look all right. I ate in the restaurant four times in all and I had a few drinks from the poolside bar. But what's this T-E-L S-T-D? That's a lot of money.

Cashier That stands for Telephone, Subscriber Trunk Dialling. That's for long distance calls that you make yourself, without the help of an operator.

Brown Yes, but I've only been here for five days and I've only spent a little time on the phone.

Cashier Have you made any international calls, Ms Brown? They're rather expensive.

Brown Well, yes, I phoned London twice and I rang a friend in Seattle the day before yesterday. But they were all short calls, two or three minutes at the most.

Cashier Well, I'll check the meter reading for you, if you like.
Brown Yes, that's a good idea. . . .
Cashier . . . No, there's no mistake. 528 units at 5 pesos. That's 2640 pesos.

Brown I didn't know it was so expensive to make calls from here. I wanted to pay the bill in cash but I haven't got enough on me. Will traveller's cheques be all right?
Cashier Yes, of course.

Listening check

1 Where on the bill is the amount that Ms Brown must pay?
2 What services did Ms Brown sign for?
3 How long has Ms Brown been at the hotel?
4 What is the abbreviation for long distance calls that you make yourself?
5 How many international calls did Ms Brown make?

Language study

Past time

Notice how we use the Past Tense for events that finished at a definite time in the past. We can use the Present Perfect Tense for events which began in the past but have not yet finished.

Mrs Wilson **checked out** of the hotel on **2 April/six days ago**.
The tour leader **has known** the hotel manager **since 1977/for six years**.

Now write out the following sentences in full, using the Past or the Present Perfect.

1 Mr Suarez (be) in Acapulco since Monday.
2 Mrs Wilson (leave) for Dubai on 17 August.
3 The Chester family (check in) on Monday afternoon.
4 Mr Villa (not visit) us since last year.
5 The Sunways tour group (spend) a week here last month.
6 They (come), as agreed, on the first of the month.
7 Ramitel Ltd (not pay) its account for the past three months.
8 Mr Lacey (be) tired after his long flight.
9 He (like) tortillas since his first visit to Mexico.
10 The tour group confirmation (not arrive) last Thursday.

Quantity

Adjectives such as **many/a lot of**, **some**, **a few** and **few** are used before things we can count. For example:

There were **many mistakes** in the guests' bill.

Adjectives such as **much/a lot of**, **some**, **a little** and **little** are used before things we cannot count. For example:

Did you spend **much money** on telephone calls?

We can show this information in the following diagram.

countable	not countable	
many/a lot of	much/a lot of	
some	some	GREATER
a few	a little	QUANTITY
few	little	

Now choose an appropriate word from the list below to complete the following sentences.

1 There is little ... about hotel services in the Key Card.
2 How much ... do you want to exchange for francs?
3 He spent a few ... checking his bill.
4 The guests didn't drink much ... during dinner.
5 There were many new ... at the hotel this year.
6 Did the tour leader have much ... with complaints from this group?
7 The brochure only gives a few ... about the coach tour.
8 The hotel received few ... about its services.

facilities	pounds
information	British currency
complaints	beer
worries	time
equipment	details
minutes	trouble
bottles of wine	

Calculating

Notice how we can express the following mathematical signs and symbols.

=	equals, is equal to, makes
−	minus, less, take away
×	multiplied by, times
$\frac{11}{16}$	eleven sixteenths
10,206	ten thousand two hundred and six
+	plus, and
÷	divided by
$\frac{3}{4}$	three quarters
$\frac{2}{3}$	two thirds
10.206	ten point two oh six

Now write out the following in words and then say them aloud.

1 120+46−92=74
2 14.135
3 $\frac{7}{8}+\frac{3}{4}=1\frac{5}{8}$
4 $4\frac{1}{2}\times2=9$
5 16,720

6 9.3÷3.1=3
7 $2\frac{1}{4}$%
8 9×3=27
9 10.5%
10 18.715

Listening and Speaking

Three customers are paying their bills. While you are listening to their conversations, complete the table below.

customer	type of service	total cost	method of payment
1 Mr Farr	food	400 + 15%	credit
2	hotel		
3			traveller's cheques

Dialogue 1

Waiter Did you enjoy your meal, Mr Farr?

Customer Yes, it was very nice indeed. I haven't eaten so well for years. Could I have the bill now, please?

Waiter Certainly, sir. I have it ready here.

Customer Ah, thank you. Tell me, is this the total amount here?

Waiter No, sir. That four hundred pesos is for your food and wine. Then there's an extra fifteen per cent service charge. The total charge is here.

Customer Good. I see. Do you accept credit cards? I've only got a little cash with me.

Waiter That's no problem. If you let me have your card, I'll get the sales voucher for your signature.

Customer Good. There's no hurry. I'll just finish my cigar.

Dialogue 2

Receptionist Good morning, Mr Johnson.

Guest Good morning. Is my bill ready?

Receptionist Yes. Here is your bill and an allowance slip as well.

Guest Sorry, could you explain what this means?

Receptionist This is an allowance slip for five hundred and fifteen pesos. You see, there was a mistake in your bill.

Guest Fine. And this is the bill then?

Receptionist That's right. It's for one thousand seven hundred and fifty five pesos. And we have to deduct the five hundred and fifteen pesos from that amount.

Guest OK. It all seems in order.

Receptionist How do you want to pay the bill?

Guest In cash.

Receptionist In pesos?

Guest Yes.

Receptionist Right. One moment and I'll write out a receipt.

Dialogue 3

Counter clerk Good afternoon, madam. Can I help you?

Customer Yes, please. I made a telephone booking for your two-day coach tour of Mexico City and Guadalajara.

Counter clerk Right. Could you give me your name, please?

Customer Of course. It's Mrs Bloom. I'm staying at the Hotel Pacific.

Counter clerk When did you make the booking?

Customer Let me see. It was two days ago.

Counter clerk Yes, here we are. For Friday and Saturday of this week.

Customer That's it. Now, is it possible to make that two tickets? I have a friend who would like to come along as well.

Counter clerk Yes, that's no problem. There are two seats together.

Customer OK. Can I pay now?

Counter Clerk Of course. The total cost of the tour is three thousand pesos per person. Are you paying for both tickets?

Customer Yes, for both. Do you take American traveller's cheques?

Counter clerk Yes, Mrs Bloom. I'll work out the exchange rate for you.

Speaking
Making calculations

Study the examples below. Notice that the cashier's first two replies are provided.

Guest Could you tell me how much it is?   (£120 − 10% = £108)
Cashier *It's a hundred and twenty pounds less ten per cent, which makes one hundred and eight pounds.*

Guest How much is it?   (D.Kr. 560 × 3 + 12½% = D.Kr. 1890)
Cashier *It's five hundred and sixty Danish crowns times three plus twelve and a half per cent, which makes one thousand eight hundred and ninety Danish crowns.*

Now do the exercise on the tape, making the Cashier's calculations in a similar way, using the information provided.

Guest What does it come to?
Cashier (DM36 + DM72 + DM13 = DM121)

Guest How much is it each?
Cashier (1105 Fr ÷ 2 = 552½ Fr)

Guest What is the total?
Cashier (21.6 − 17.3 = 4.3)

Guest What does it come to?
Cashier (46,150 L − 2% = 45,227 L)

Guest How much is it?
Cashier ($340 + $291 − $33½ = $597½)

Activities

Activity A

Five guests are checking out of the Hotel del Golfo. Details are given about their bills and methods of payment. Decide how much change each of them should get. The foreign exchange table below will help you. The rates are given in Mexican pesos.

country	currency		cash	traveller's cheques
France	Franc	(1)	4.5	4.8
Germany (West)	DM	(1)	10.6	11.0
Italy	Lire	(100)	2.4	–
Japan	Yen	(100)	10.5	11.0
Saudi Arabia	Rial	(1)	7.4	–
Spain	Pta	(100)	29.7	–
UK	£	(1)	51.5	53.0
USA	$	(1)	23.5	24.0

Example:

Miss Forbes The total amount payable on her bill is 6480 pesos, but the hotel has billed her wrongly for a meal costing 810 pesos. Deduct this. She pays with three £50 traveller's cheques.

▶ 6480 pesos less 810 pesos equals 5670 pesos. £150 at the traveller's cheque rate is 150 times 53 pesos. That makes 7950 pesos. The change she should get is 7950 minus 5670 pesos. That comes to 2280 pesos.

In a similar way, write out the calculations for the change that should be given to these guests.

Ms Lamondou Her bill totals 3900 pesos and she wishes to pay it with a 1000 franc note.

Mr Duensing His bill comes to 12,960 pesos. He is given a 10% discount on this. He pays with eleven 100 DM traveller's cheques.

Mr Ayyad His bill amounts to 5075 pesos. 15% service charge must be added to this amount. He pays with 1000 Rials, in cash.

Mr and Mrs Ruiz Their bill totals 20,140 pesos, less 670 pesos for an allowance slip. They wish to pay with seven 10,000 peseta notes.

Activity B

Look at the tariff for the Hotel Maya and the list of some of the guests in residence.

Hotel Maya – Tariff	
Single Bedroom	1900 pesos, per person
Double/Twin Bedroom	1300 ,,　　　 ,,
Private Bathroom	400 ,,　　　 ,,
Inclusive Terms	2600 ,,　　　 ,,
Table d'hôte Lunch	450 ,,　　　 ,,

Notes (i) the room rate includes breakfast
(ii) the rates include tax and service charge
(iii) inclusive terms cover room, breakfast, lunch, and dinner

room number	type	name
301	Single and Bath	Mr P Landseer
302	Single	Miss O Santiago
303	Double	Mr and Mrs F Craig
304	Double and Bath	Mr and Mrs L Saunders
305	Single – Inclusive	Mr J Jules

Now study the following list of services provided for these guests on 23.8.82.

07.00 Newspapers: Room 303 – 25 pesos   Room 305 – 50 pesos
08.15 Telephone calls: Mrs Craig – 225 pesos   Mr Saunders – 25 pesos
09.00 Flowers: Room 304 – 425 pesos
09.30 Hairdresser: Miss Santiago – 550 pesos
10.00 Coffee Shop: Room 302 – 200 pesos   Room 305 – 315 pesos
11.00 Taxi: Room 304 – 940 pesos
11.15 Theatre Ticket: Room 303 – 300 pesos
11.45 Bar: Room 301 – 160 pesos   Room 302 – 215 pesos
12.30 Lunch: Mr Landseer   Mr and Mrs Craig
14.00 Kiosk: Room 305 – 175 pesos
15.30 Coffee Shop: Mr Saunders – 300 pesos   Mr Landseer – 200 pesos
16.15 Laundry: Room 302 – 430 pesos
17.00 Car Hire: Room 303 – 1930 pesos
17.45 Bar: Room 303 – 275 pesos   Room 304 – 225 pesos
20.30 Restaurant: Mr Landseer – 530 pesos

Calculate the amount payable by each room for 23.8.82.

Writing

Notice how the following pairs of sentences are linked using **and/as well as**, **so/therefore** and **but/however**.

Examples:

Bills in that restaurant include service. They also include VAT.
▶ Bills in that restaurant include service **and** VAT.
▶ Bills in that restaurant include service **as well as** VAT.

The hotel forgot to add the service charge. He paid less than he expected.
▶ The hotel forgot to add the service charge, **so** he paid less than he expected.
▶ The hotel forgot to add the service charge. **Therefore** he paid less than he expected.

They sent a letter of confirmation. It was lost in the post.
▶ They sent a letter of confirmation, **but** it was lost in the post.
▶ They sent a letter of confirmation. **However**, it was lost in the post.

Note that 'therefore' and 'however' are usually used to begin a new sentence. They are more formal than 'so' and 'but'. After 'however' we usually add a comma.

Link the following pairs of sentences using **and/as well as** or **so/therefore** or **but/however.**

1 You can buy whisky in town. It's cheaper at the airport.
2 They didn't have any cash on them. They had to use their credit cards.
3 The sightseeing trip goes through the old quarter. It also goes through the modern city centre.
4 There is a radio in the room. There is a colour TV, too.

Now link the sentences in the following passage.

When Mr Landseer arrived at the airport he wanted to hire a car ... the cost was rather high. He did not have enough cash on him ... he decided to use his credit card. Unfortunately when he felt in his pocket he found that his wallet was missing. His cheque book was missing, too. ... he did have his agent's telephone number ... he was able to ring for help.

Word study

amount p. 96, quantity.
automatically p. 96, without special instructions; by itself.
calculate p. 96, compute; work out. *n* **calculation** and **calculator**.

calculator

change p. 96, if my bill is £92 and I give the cashier £95, I should receive £3 change.
control p. 94, direction; supervision. *v* **control**.
development p. 94, growth and advancement. *v* **develop**.
discount p. 101, amount deducted from the price for reasons such as quick payment or cash payment.
exchange rate p. 96, amount of one currency that can be obtained for an amount of another.
financial p. 94, concerning money. The noun and verb are **finance**.
guarantee p. 96, be sure of. *n* **guarantee**.
itemized p. 96, detailed. *n* **item**.
ledger account p. 96, account paid at a fixed time, for example, the end of the month.
machine billing p. 94, producing bills on, for example, NCR or Sweda machines.

makes p. 100, equals; comes to.
memory p. 96, store of information.
meter p. 97.

on me p. 97, in my possession now.
payable p. 101, which should be
    paid.
pool p. 96, this is a shorter way of
    saying **swimming pool**.
post p. 96, record.
printed out p. 95, produced in a
    written form.
programmed p. 96, instructed.
    n **program**.
reduce p. 96, make less; decrease.
    n **reduction**.
running total p. 96, current total.
sales ledger p. 96, statement of sales.
sales voucher p. 99, receipt when
    credit card is used.
settle p. 95, pay.
tabular ledger p. 94, book for
    recording charges.
units p. 97, see **meter**.
up to date p. 94, current.

Revision Unit 2

The exercises in this unit are revision of some of the work studied in Units 5–8 of the course.

1 Prepositions

Complete the sentences below with appropriate prepositions from the following list: **from**, **at**, **on**, **over**, **with**, **in**, **to**, **off** and **after**.

1 The Paris train departs ... the Central Station ... six o'clock.
2 I'll meet you ... the reception desk ... I have finished my dinner.
3 Mr Lampard requested a room ... the fourth floor ... a view that looked ... the park.
4 The Coffee Shop is open ... eight ... the morning ... eleven ... night.
5 The hotel is situated ... the Avenue Fouret which is just ... the main street.
6 For the Post Office, you take the second ... your left and the first ... your right.
7 She always stays ... the same hotel ... the city centre.
8 Can I pay my bill ... traveller's cheques?

2 Vocabulary

Choose the correct word from those in the brackets in order to complete the following sentences.

1 One of the gueridon waiter's (works/tasks/procedures) is to carve meat on the trolley.
2 The Weekly Guide gives details of all the main tourist (events/admissions/accompaniments) in the city.
3 We bought a number of (souvenirs/resorts/occasions) in the covered market.
4 Three nights at £34 a night (calculates/works out/comes to) £102.
5 The telephone calls for each room are recorded on a (clock/meter/calculator).
6 For (starters/apéritifs/introductions), they chose melon and grapefruit.
7 STD (stands for/abbreviates/shows) subscriber trunk dialling.
8 The hotel has introduced a (self-served/self-help/self-service) system at lunch time.

3 Flow chart

Use the information below to complete the following flow chart of a guest's stay at an hotel.

a. Allocate room
b. Guest departs
c. Goes to room
d. Pays bill
e. Inform departments of arrival
f. Open bill
g. Pass mail and messages

h. Post charges
i. Inform departments of departure
j. Check registration card
k. Check charges and close bill
l. Receive room back to re-let
m. Registration
n. Uses hotel facilities

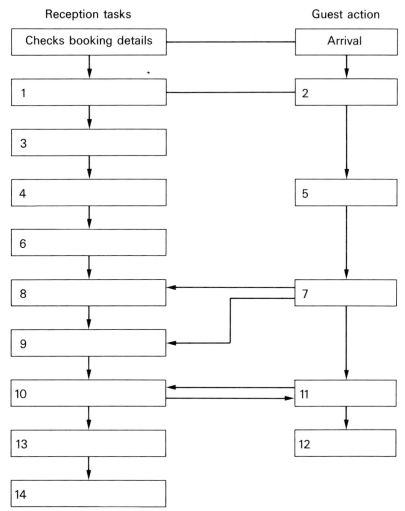

Reception tasks

Guest action

| Checks booking details | | Arrival |

1 — 2

3

4   5

6

8 ← 7

9 ←

10 ← 11 →

13   12

14

Flow chart of guest stay

4 Verb tenses and forms

In the following sentences, place the word(s) in brackets in the correct tense and/or form.

1 Mr Joel ... for the airport ten minutes ago. (leave)
2 The Sun Tour group ... two hours ago but they were delayed in Barcelona. (should arrive)
3 The Hotel Concord ... a new night club next Saturday night. (open)
4 If you would like to take a seat, I ... your bill. (calculate)
5 The weather ... very good since the beginning of last week. (be)
6 Because of a breakdown, the passengers ... to another coach last night. (transfer)
7 We ... the tabular ledger since 1976. (not use)
8 The next London train ... from platform seven at 21.30. (depart)
9 A picnic lunch ... when we visit the medieval cathedral at Chartres tomorrow. (provide)
10 Money ... to the customer who complained about the tour. (not refund)

5 Multiple choice

Complete the following sentences in an appropriate way.

1 When a customer who is known to be difficult comes into a restaurant he should be

   a. given better service than the other customers.
   b. given larger amounts of food than the other customers.
   c. served with care by an experienced waiter.
   d. refused admission.

2 If the day's total receipts including VAT @ 15% are £4764.20, the receipts exclusive of VAT are

   a. £4142.78
   b. £4284.00
   c. £4301.62
   d. £4321.16

3 With silver service, the menu is usually

   a. à la carte.
   b. table d'hôte.
   c. either à la carte or table d'hôte.

4 The correct way to express eleven thousand three hundred and fifty-six in English is

   a. 11 356
   b. 11,356
   c. 11.356

5 If a headwaiter receives a complaint of poor service from a customer, he should apologize to the customer and

   a. immediately inform the manager.
   b. make an excuse to the customer.
   c. speak to the waiter concerned.
   d. ask the waiter for his comments before replying to the customer.

6 A tabular ledger is

   a. a type of computerized bill.
   b. a machine billing system.
   c. a written method of recording charges.
   d. a list of guests' payments.

6 Translation

Translate the following words and expressions into your own language.

1 a. chips, b. soft drinks, c. picnic lunch, d. mineral water.
2 a. well done, b. rare, c. spicy, d. filleted.
3 a. nightlife, b. floor show, c. sunbathing, d. fishing.
4 a. brochure, b. holiday guide, c. map, d. magazine.
5 a. delay, b. overbooking, c. transfer, d. refund.
6 a. change, b. ledger account, c. billing machine, d. itemized bill.

7 Verbs and nouns

Complete the following table.

verb	noun	verb	noun
1 refund	......	9 develop	......
2	calculation	10	transfer
3 entertain	......	11	finance
4	item	12 apologize	......
5	guide	13 inhabit	......
6	economy	14 advertise	......
7 diet	......	15	comment
8 state	......	16 reduce	......

8 Letter writing

Using the information below, write three letters of reply as the manager of the Hotel International. Choose an appropriate date and address.

1 Mr and Mrs Sykes of 32 Dean Street, Wolverhampton, England have written to the Hotel International requesting a twin-bedded room with a bath for 7 nights from 16.9.82. However, a twin-bedded room with bath is available only from 17.9.82. Alternatively, the Bristol Hotel, a nearby hotel of similar standard and price, is recommended.

2 Mr Jon Rogers, the Secretary of the Bath Social Club, 7 Walmer Crescent, Bath, England would like to book the Atlantic Room for a dinner and dance for 32 persons for the night 17.10.82. Unfortunately, the Atlantic Room is not available. However, the Terrace Suite at the International is available on that night at the same rates.

3 Miss E Straw, Fairview, High Street, Woland, Buckinghamshire, England has written to complain of poor Floor and Reception service; slow food service; and an overcharge on her bill during her recent stay.

9 Description

Answer the following questions.

1 Explain the difference between
   a. a ledger account and a sales ledger
   b. a refund and an allowance
   c. a discount and a reduced rate
   d. the exchange rate and change

2 Describe four types of food service.

3 You are working in Reception when a customer complains loudly about the poor service he is receiving in the hotel. What do you do?

4 List the kind of information that a Hall Porter should be able to provide hotel guests.

5 Describe six methods of payment.

Study the exchange rate table and the paying-in sheet below. The Cashier has made a number of mistakes in his calculations on the paying-in sheet. Find these mistakes and correct them.

Exchange rate table for sterling.

country	currency	cash	traveller's cheques
Canada	Canada $	2.64	2.615
France	Franc	11.46	11.23
Germany (West)	DM	4.89	4.76
Italy	Lire	2390	2380
Japan	Yen	492	473
Switzerland	Franc	4.45	4.34
Netherlands	Guilder	5.41	5.28

Paying-in sheet

foreign payments		
currency	amount	sterling total
1 Japanese TC	16,555	35.00
2 Dutch N	200	35.78
3 Canadian N	261.50	100.00
4 German TC	650	139.20
5 Italian N	76,000	31.80
6 Swiss TC	800	179.78
7 Dutch TC	1720	325.76
8 Swiss N	800	178.79
9 French N	1000	89.05
10 Canadian TC	250	96.50
	Total £1226.64	

N = notes
TC = traveller's cheques

Unit 9
Tour operation – Contacts

Reading and Listening

Reading

There have been a number of developments in the UK tourist market in recent years. The International Passenger Survey (IPS) on the next page shows how different segments of the market have been affected.

The changing composition of travel segments			
	Volume %		
	1977	1978	1979
Miscellaneous, incl. studies	17.6	18.1	18.5
Business	17.4	18.1	18.8
Holidays/Leisure	65.0	63.8	62.7
Analysis of leisure travel:			
Holiday inclusive	23.3	20.1	18.6
Holiday independent	51.2	52.7	52.4
Visiting friends and relatives	25.5	27.2	29.0

British Tourist Authority statistics

Since 1973, the number of inclusive tours to Britain has fallen. There are various reasons for this trend. There has been (1) an increase in motoring traffic, (2) an increase in the volume of repeat visitors who make their own ground arrangements, and (3) an increase in the availability of promotional fares.

Further availability of promotional fares such as standbys and walk-on services will be significant. Fares may become so low that the trend to independent ravel is accelerated. On the other hand, if group accommodation was supplied at more attractive rates and if new markets were expanded, this would produce a stronger demand for inclusive holidays.

However, the message is clear. UK tourist boards, tour operators, and hoteliers need to create a demand for their products and sell them abroad. They have to go out and make contacts at travel trade exhibitions and workshops and put together inclusive tours with appeal in different markets.

When preparing an inclusive tour, the essential first step is to obtain attractive group rates and schedulings from a carrier. Then, familiarization trips can be held for interested tour operators and travel agents who are capable of organizing flight inclusive tours (FITs).

Finally, when a tour operator decides to launch a new package, it is necessary to invite travel trade journalists and travel agency staff to the area in order to view the product.

Reading check

1 By how many per cent did holiday-inclusive travel fall in the UK between 1977 and 1979?
2 Name two types of promotional fare.
3 What factors will have an effect on the future of inclusive holidays?
4 What kind of people are invited on familiarization trips?
5 Who is invited to an area before a new product is launched?

Judith Wilkinson is at the Yorkshire and Humberside Tourist Board stand at the 1982 International Tourism Exchange in Berlin. Listen to her establishing contact with a visitor who is looking at the photographic display.

Wilkinson Those are photographs of the Dales region in Yorkshire. You may have seen the BBC programmes about the life of a veterinary surgeon in the area. They've been widely exported.

Van de Veen Yes, I have seen two or three of the programmes. It's certainly beautiful country.

Wilkinson It is, isn't it? I don't think we've met before. My name's Judith Wilkinson. I'm Assistant Commercial Manager with the Board.

Van de Veen Pleased to meet you, Ms Wilkinson. I'm Joos van de Veen. Here's my card.

Wilkinson Ah yes, I see you're with Nederlandtour.

Van de Veen Yes. I'm the Regional Manager for the central Netherlands, based in Utrecht. Perhaps you know Piet Boonstra from our head office in Amsterdam? He usually deals with northern Britain.

Wilkinson Yes. I did meet him once in London.

Van de Veen Yes, that BBC series has given you very good publicity. In fact it's been such a success that interest in Yorkshire has grown significantly.

Wilkinson Well, we'd be very happy if that interest resulted in an increase in demand. Do you foresee a rise in numbers from the central Netherlands?

Van de Veen Yes, I think so. The business sector will probably remain the same. But I'm expecting considerable growth in both the inclusive and the independent sectors.

Wilkinson Well, we certainly have a lot to offer, and not just beautiful countryside. We have interesting historic cities, such as York; a long coastline; a wide range of activity and special interest holidays; and types of accommodation to suit every preference and budget.

Van de Veen Fine. Perhaps we could discuss some of these things in a bit more detail . . .

1 What is Judith Wilkinson's job?
2 Where does Mr van de Veen have his office?
3 Where has Ms Wilkinson met Mr van de Veen's colleague?
4 Which type of visit from the central Netherlands will probably not increase?
5 What sort of accommodation is available in Yorkshire and Humberside?

Language study

Cause and effect

Study the table below.

year	cause	effect
1 1974	a great increase in fuel costs	inclusive tours became much dearer
2 1976	a high occupancy level	group rates were not attractive
3 1977	a heavy demand for tours	overbooking became a problem
4 1978	a hot summer	fewer people went abroad
5 1979	a sudden reduction in fares	independent travel was more popular
6 1981	a popular BBC series	more people went to Yorkshire

Now look at the following examples and notice how we can link the cause and effect using **so** ... **that** or **such** ... **that**.

In 1974, there was **such** a great increase in fuel costs **that** inclusive tours became much dearer.

In 1974, the increase in fuel costs was **so** great **that** inclusive tours became much dearer.

Now link cause and effect in examples 2–6 in a similar way.

Using statistics

Study the following bar chart. It shows the proportion of overseas visitors compared to the total number of guests in a London hotel.

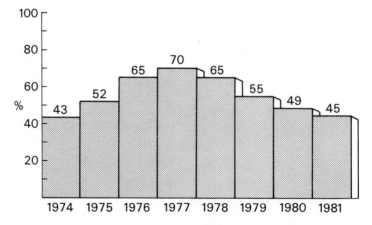

Proportion of overseas visitors in a London hotel

Notice how we can express information about the chart in two ways.
Between 1974–75, the proportion of overseas visitors **increased by 9%**.

or Between 1974–75, there was **a 9% increase** in the proportion of overseas visitors.

In a similar way, provide alternatives for the following sentences.

1 From 1975 to 1976, the proportion of overseas visitors rose by 14%.
2 Between 1974 and 1977, there was a 27% expansion in the proportion of overseas visitors.
3 There was an increase in the proportion of overseas visitors from 52% to 70% between 1975 and 1977.
4 Between 1975 and 1977, the proportion of overseas visitors grew by 18%.
5 The proportion of overseas visitors has fallen by 4% since last year.
6 The proportion of overseas visitors decreased from 70% to 65% between 1977 and 1978.

Considering future possibilities

Examples:

What **would happen** if promotional fares **were increased**? (amount of independent travel/decrease)
▶ If promotional fares **were increased**, the amount of independent travel **would decrease**.

What **would happen** if hoteliers **put up** group rates? (demand for accommodation/fall)
▶ Demand for accommodation **would fall**, if hoteliers **put up** group rates.

Now answer the following in a similar way.

1 What would happen if fuel prices were reduced? (number of motoring holidays/rise)
   ▶ If ...
2 What would be the result if the value of the pound was lower? (British holidays/become more popular)
   ▶ British holidays ...
3 What would happen if tourists complained more? (standards of service/improve)
   ▶ If ...
4 What would be the effect if fewer people in the UK went on package tours abroad? (domestic resorts/benefit)
   ▶ Domestic resorts ...
5 What would happen if the economic situation did not improve? (tourism/not expand rapidly)
   ▶ Tourism ...
6 What would be the result if areas were not advertised? (level of tourist activity/not grow significantly)
   ▶ If ...

Listening and Speaking

Listening

Judith Wilkinson has two telephone calls to make. While you are listening to the conversations, complete the table below.

to: name position	day and time of meeting	place of meeting	subject for discussion
Harry Dent Commercial Manager	1	UK Airways London office	2
Mr Cotton 3	4	5	6

Dialogue 1

Operator UK Airways, good morning.
Wilkinson Good morning. Could I speak to the Commercial Manager, please?
Operator That's extension 472. Hold the line, please.
Dent Hallo, Harry Dent here.
Wilkinson Hallo, Harry. This is Judith Wilkinson from the Yorkshire and Humberside Tourist Board.
Dent Ah, Judith. What can I do for you?
Wilkinson Do you remember our discussion about the possibility of fortnightly flights into Leeds/Bradford from Copenhagen?
Dent Yes, of course. We do have the aircraft available on the dates you mentioned. And, as I said, there would only be a fifteen per cent increase on last year's rates.
Wilkinson Good. We're hoping to approach a number of Danish tour operators in the near future. But before we do that, I'd like to meet you in order to finalize our arrangements and get it all on paper.
Dent Fine. What about next week? I'm so busy at the moment that this week is out of the question.
Wilkinson Well, I'll be in London next Tuesday. I'm at European Ferry Lines in the morning. How about some time after lunch? Two thirty, say?

Dent Ah, two thirty is a little early for me. I have someone coming at two. Could we make it three, perhaps? Or would that be too late?
Wilkinson No, three would be fine. If I leave your office at about four thirty, I'll be able to get the five o'clock train. OK. I'll see you on Tuesday, then.
Dent Right. Goodbye for now.
Wilkinson Goodbye.

Dialogue 2

Operator Good morning. White Rose Hotel. Can I help you?
Wilkinson Yes, I'd like to speak to the General Manager, please.
Operator Just one moment.
Secretary Hello. This is Mr Cotton's secretary speaking.
Wilkinson This is Judith Wilkinson from the Tourist Board. Is Mr Cotton there, please?
Secretary One moment, please.
Cotton Hello, Cotton here.
Wilkinson Hello, Mr Cotton. It's Judith Wilkinson.
Cotton Ah, Mrs Wilkinson. What can I do for you?
Wilkinson You remember our discussions about the eastern United States. Well, there's been such a lot of interest that we are thinking of organizing a trip for various tour operators.

Cotton Good idea. It would be nice if we had more visitors from the States. We do seem to get fewer and fewer these days.

Wilkinson Yes. They are particularly interested in up-market, traditional accommodation such as yours. Do you think we could meet to discuss arrangements for a visit of tour operators to your hotel?

Cotton Most certainly. When would you like to come?

Wilkinson Is next Monday at ten convenient?

Cotton That suits me fine.

Wilkinson Right. I'll see you next week.

Cotton Fine. Goodbye, Mrs Wilkinson.

Speaking
Giving emphasis

Notice in the first two examples below how the verb is emphasized using **do** and **did**.

Product Manager I **saw** Mr Angelo in Rome last week.
Product Manager *I did see Mr Angelo in Rome last week.*

Product Manager I **like** the new UK brochure.
Product Manager *I do like the new UK brochure.*

Now do the exercise on the tape, emphasizing the verbs in a similar way.

Product Manager We found their prices were significantly higher.
Product Manager Mr McKay expects you to arrive tomorrow.
Product Manager I remembered to contact the Commercial Manager.
Product Manager I think we need more publicity.
Product Manager We plan to extend our inclusive tours programme.

Activities

Activity A

Study the advertisement on the next page and answer the questions below.

1 Where can you obtain free information folders?
2 Who qualifies for Railcards?
3 What does the cost of a Golden Rail package include?
4 What types of return fare are available from British Rail?
5 At what UK address can overseas visitors get information?
6 What is the maximum time during which you can use a Britrail Pass?

A GREAT WAY TO SEE GREAT BRITAIN

Some ways to cut the cost

Depending on when you travel and how long you stay, Special Fare Deals can save you a lot of money on fares to and around Yorkshire and Humberside. Choose from Awayday, Weekend, Monthly and Ordinary Returns. Or you may qualify for a Railcard which gives even greater savings – Family, Senior Citizen and Student Railcards are available.

Yorkshire Ranger Ticket

This special ticket allows you seven days' unlimited travel during summer within the area. Ask for the free folder giving details.

Golden Rail

Package holidays which are easy to book and give value for money – you choose to suit your budget from a four-star hotel to accommodation with families. The inclusive tour covers Inter-City travel from anywhere in Britain, reserved seats on most trains, transport between the resort station and hotel and, where appropriate, across London.

Britrail Pass

Special cheap rate season tickets are available for American and European visitors. There's a pass to suit your travel requirements – from seven consecutive days to one month, giving unlimited travel to any station in the British Isles. A Britrail pass must be bought in the visitor's own country.

How to get your free folders

There are free folders detailing the fares and facilities mentioned here. Pick up the ones you're interested in from your local Inter-City station or a British Rail Appointed Travel Agent. Overseas visitors can find out more about rail services and facilities by contacting Britrail Travel International Inc, 630 Third Avenue, New York NY 10017, U.S.A. or Britrail Travel International Inc, 222 Marylebone Road, London NW1 6JJ.

Activity B

When we look at the UK tourist market for overseas visitors, we can consider (a) the number of visits made by people from different areas and (b) the amount of money spent during these visits. In the table below, these two factors are expressed as percentages of the total number of visits and of the total expenditure.

1979 Actual Share of Visits and Expenditure		
Expenditure	Country/area	Visits
1	6	1%
6%	Scandinavia	8%
2	7	13%
10%	Central Europe	16%
5%	8	13 ......
3	Italy/Spain/Portugal	14 ......
3%	Eastern Europe	2%
3%	9	15 ......
4	10	13%
4%	11	16 ......
5	12	4%

British Tourist Authority and Department of Industry statistics

1 Now use the following information to complete the table.

Visitors to the UK from neighbouring countries had a higher percentage of total visits compared to their percentage of total expenditure. For example, people from Benelux made 13% of the visits to the UK but only spent 7% of the total. The figures for France were both 2% lower than the Benelux figures. For Eire, the figure for visits was 7% with 4% less for expenditure.

For more distant European countries and North America, the visits and expenditure percentages are much closer. Taking visits first, the figures for Italy/Spain/Portugal were 6% and 5%. For the USA, they were 13% and 15% and for Canada 4% each.

Long-haul visitors, on the other hand, had a higher percentage for expenditure than for the visits. For Australia/New Zealand, the visits figure was 4% with 3% more for expenditure. Japanese visitors made 1% of the visits but their percentage of expenditure was double this.

2 Visitors from neighbouring countries make more visits but spend less. Long-haul visitors come less frequently but spend more. What is the explanation for this, do you think?

Writing

In the two telexes below, the following abbreviations are used.

ASAP – as soon as possible   EEE – error
PLS – please   ATTN – attention
TLX – telex   RE – concerning
OCC – subscriber is engaged

Read the telexes and answer the questions that follow.

```
12.57    OCC

13.15    57715 YORHTB G
         27143 EFL G

14.05.82

ATTN    TONY JOHNSON
RE      YORKSHIRE BROCHURES

COULD YOU PLS SEND US ASAP 200 GERMAN AND 21 EEE 200 DUTCH
COPU EEE COPIES OF THE NEW YORKSHIRE BROCHURE.
PLS ADVISE US BY TLX THAT YOU HAVE SENT THEM TO OUR HULL
OFFICE FOR THE ATTN OF MR JAMES.
THANK YOU IN ADVANCE
REGARDS
EUROPEAN FERRY LINES
JOHN CARSTAIRS

27143 EFL G
57715 YORHTB G
```

```
11.30    27143 EFL G
         57715 YORHTB G
15.05.82

ATTN    JOHN CARSTAIRS
HERE YORKSHIRE AND HUMBERSIDE TOURIST BOARD. RE YOUR TLX
14.05.82. BROCHURES YOU REQUESTED HAVE BEEN SENT TO MR JAMES
AT HULL TODAY.
REGARDS
JOHNSON

57715 YORHTB G
27143 EFL G
```

1 What has Mr Carstairs requested from Mr Johnson?
2 Who does Mr Johnson work for?
3 At what time did John Carstairs first try to contact John Carlton?
4 On what date were the brochures sent?
5 What is European Ferry Lines' telex number?

Writing B

Using the telex number for the Yorkshire and Humberside Tourist Board as above, write out the following telex messages. Choose an appropriate time and date for each message.

1 ● Maria Baan of Delft Tour (tlx. 61789 DT NL) has requested 5 copies of 'Where to stay in Yorkshire' for her head office.
  ● Tony Johnson has replied that 'Where to stay in Yorkshire' is not available until next week. He will send copies then.

2 ● John Gould of International Tourist Monthly (tlx. 41263 IT G) has informed the Board that the party of German journalists expected at Hull at 22.00 on 23.6.82 will not arrive until the following morning at 6.30. Mr Gould has asked if the Board's representative will be able to meet the party at the new time.
  ● Mr Johnson has replied to confirm the new time for meeting the party.

3 ● Paul Belmonde of Beltour (tlx. 52369 BEL B) has requested information on the availability of tour guides and their rates for half- and full-day sightseeing in York.
  ● Mr Johnson has replied that guides are available from 1 May until 31 October. The rates are £30 for a full day and £20 for a half-day. The maximum number in a group is 15 people.

Word study

accelerated p. 112, made quicker.
appointed p. 118, chosen.
based p. 113, located.
budget p. 113, financial plan.
  v **budget**.
card p. 113.

YORKSHIRE & HUMBERSIDE TOURIST BOARD
312 Tadcaster Rd . York YO2 2HF Tel. York (0904) 707961 Telex 57715

Jane Wylde
Commercial Manager

A visiting card

carrier p. 112, transport company, eg airline, ferry company.
consecutive days p. 118, one after the other: ie Monday, Tuesday, Wednesday.

create p. 112, make.
demand p. 112, amount people wish to buy. v **demand**.
essential p. 112, necessary.
expansion p. 115, increase in size; growth. v **expand**.
expenditure p. 119, money spent.
exported p. 113, sold abroad. The opposite is **imported**.
ground arrangements p. 112, arrangements made at the destination such as booking hotels, hiring cars.
factors p. 112, facts of particular importance.
familiarization trips p. 112, trips for people in the tourist industry to get to know and inspect an area and the services available. The short form is **FAMs**.

fares p. 112, prices of travel tickets.

flight inclusive tours p. 112, tours which include cost of flight, transfers, accommodation, etc.

foresee p. 113, expect; anticipate.

fuel p. 114, petrol, oil etc.

independent travel p. 112, holidays for which people make their own travel and accommodation arrangements.

journalists p. 112, people who write for newspapers and magazines.

launch p. 112, introduce on the market. *n* **launch**.

long-haul p. 119, long distance.

package p. 112, inclusive tour.

promotional fares p. 112, special cheap fares.

proportion p. 114, comparative part.

publicity p. 113, information that gets people interested.

qualify p. 118, meet the requirements.

region p. 113, area of a country.

repeat visitors p. 112, visitors who return to the same place.

segment p. 111, part; sector.

senior citizen p. 118, man over 65, woman over 60 years old.

significant p. 112, full of meaning; important.

standbys p. 112, unreserved airline tickets obtained shortly before departure.

traditional p. 117, not modern.

trend p. 112, movement.

up-market p. 117, expensive.

veterinary surgeon p. 113, doctor for animals.

volume p. 112, size.

walk-on services p. 112, air services on which seats can not be reserved.

workshops p. 112, study groups.

Unit 10
Tour operation – Familiarization

Reading and Listening

Reading

312 Tadcaster Road, York YO2 2HF
Telephone York(0904)707961 Telex 57715

Director: John Dillon-Guy
Chairman: County Cllr. Col. R. J. L. Jackson, C.B.E., D.L., J.P.
Hon Treasurer: K. R. Hounsome, County Treasurer, N.Y.C.C.
Hon Secretary: R. G. Brooke, Director of Administration, W.Y.C.C.

Our Ref: JW/1175   Your Ref: JFB/cmr

Mr J F Burwin
Managing Director
Texas Travel Inc
147-149 Smith Boulevard
Houston   11 March 1982
Texas 77085

Dear Mr Burwin

During your visit to our stand at the Berlin trade fair, we discussed
tourist interest in our part of England. We both thought it might
become a very popular destination for Texan tourists.

Recently, the Board have been discussing the possibility of organizing
FITs from Texas. We have now reached agreement with UK Airways on the
travel arrangements. As a result of this, we are preparing, in association
with the carrier, a familiarization tour of our region. We hope that
about fifteen Texas tour operators and travel agents will join the party.
We would be pleased if you would be able to participate in this tour.

The most suitable time for us is between 17 and 21 May. I am enclosing
a proposed itinerary. We would like to show you the sightseeing attractions
and introduce you to the wide range of holiday types available in the
region. We hope to include hotel packages, up-market independent tours
for seasoned travellers, escorted tours, activity holidays, and special
seasonal tours. We feel that the flight costings are so reasonable that
it should also be possible to market family-oriented low budget packages.
These might include self-catering arrangements.

We should be able to give you fuller details of the tour within the next
two weeks. In the meantime, perhaps you would be kind enough to let
us know if you would be interested in joining us and if the dates are
convenient.

Yours sincerely,

Judith Wilkinson
Assistant Commercial Manager

1 Where did Mr Burwin first make contact with the YHTB?
2 What has made it possible for the YHTB to arrange the tour?
3 Who is organizing the tour with the YHTB?
4 Who will take part in the FAM?
5 What is the purpose of the tour?
6 What would the YHTB like Mr Burwin to do before he is given more details of the tour?

Listening

Listen to the conversation between James Cooper, a tour operator, and Andrew Parks, General Manager of the Landseer Hotel.

Johnson Mr Cooper, I'd like to introduce you to Andrew Parks, manager of the Landseer.

Cooper Glad to meet you, Mr Parks.

Parks And you. How are you enjoying your trip?

Cooper I've been having a pretty interesting time. Busy, too.

Johnson Well, if you would excuse me for a while, gentlemen.

Cooper Sure, Mr Johnson. We'll see you later.

Parks Is this your first visit here, Mr Cooper?

Cooper To this part of England, yes.

Parks What's your particular interest?

Cooper Well, I have a company called Travel International. We sell a wide range of European holidays, from low budget upwards. Just now, I'm interested in something a little more traditional: good, comfortable hotels, interesting places to visit. That kind of thing.

Parks Well, we can certainly provide that.

Cooper Could you tell me a little about the Landseer?

Parks Of course. What would you like to know?

Cooper Let's start with the accommodation. How many rooms are there?

Parks We have a hundred and eighteen rooms, all with bath or shower.

Cooper What are the room types?

Parks Singles, twins, doubles and five suites.

Cooper Are the twins more expensive than the doubles?

Parks Oh no, they're the same.

Cooper How about food service?

Parks We have two restaurants and a coffee shop. And this is the Cocktail Bar, one of the four lounge bars.

Cooper That should take care of everyone's thirst. Are all the bars as comfortable as this one?

Parks Why don't we make a tour of the hotel? You could look over some of the rooms, have a chat with the chef, and get an idea of the floor and reception services.

Cooper That sounds like a good idea. There's nothing better than seeing for yourself.

1 What is the name of Mr Cooper's company?
2 What kinds of holidays is Mr Cooper interested in at the moment?
3 Name the room types at the Landseer.
4 Are the double rooms less expensive than the twins?
5 How many bars does the Landseer have?

Language study

Probability and possibility

Study the table below.

MORE CERTAIN ↑	certain	The rates **will** be higher next year.
	probable	Flight UK 412 **should** arrive on time.
	possible	He **might** come tomorrow.

Notice how we use **will**, **should**, and **might** to show how certain we are about what we are saying.

Examples:

This is possibly our final meeting.
▶ This **might** be our final meeting.

It is certain to be an interesting tour of the region.
▶ It **will** be an interesting tour of the region.

Now write sentences using **will**, **should**, and **might** in a similar way.

1 There will probably be a good price from the carrier.
2 It was very windy over Europe so it's possible the plane will be late.
3 It is likely that your letter will arrive tomorrow.
4 I'm not sure if Vista Voyages are sending a representative.
5 There are certain to be a number of problems with the schedule.
6 There is a possibility we will visit the Berlin trade fair.
7 UK 790 is due to arrive in twenty minutes.
8 There is definitely no train service on 25 December.

Past time

Study the table below.

| room | name | arr | dep | reason for visit |
		April		
101	Mrs Wilson	21	24	conference
102	Mr and Mrs Lopez	20		holiday
103	Mr Arden	24		business
104	Mr and Mrs Chester	17	24	holiday
105	Mr Suarez	22		holiday

Details of a survey of rooms 101–105 at the Minster Hotel, York, dated 27 April

Notice how we can ask questions and give answers about the table using the Past and the Present Perfect Continuous.

Examples:

When did Mrs Wilson arrive?
▶ She arrived on 21 April/six days ago.

How long has Mr Suarez been staying in York?
▶ He's been staying there since 22 April/for five days.

Now answer these questions in a similar way.
1 On what date did the Chesters leave York?
2 Since when have Mr and Mrs Lopez been occupying room 102?
3 For what reason has Mr Arden been staying in York?
4 Why did Mr and Mrs Chester come to York?
5 Who has been staying the longest in these rooms?
6 What has Mr Suarez been doing in York?

Comparing

Study the following table.

	Roebuck Hotel	White Rose Hotel	Carlton Hotel
Singles	55	37	10
Doubles	32	19	5
Twins	59	40	21
Rack rate	£30	£29.50	£27.50
Full board	£42.50	£40.75	£38
Group discount	15%	15%	20%

Notice how we can ask questions comparing the information about the hotels.

Does the Roebuck have **fewer** singles **than** twins?
Is the discount in the White Rose **as high as** in the Carlton?
Is the Carlton's rack rate **less expensive than** the Roebuck's?
Which is **the biggest** hotel?

Use the table to make ten more similar questions.

Listening and Speaking

Listening

Dan Adler, a tour operator, is discussing the services that certain companies can provide. While you are listening to his conversations, complete the table below.

name of contact	name of company	type of company	special service requested by Mr Adler
1	Rentex Ltd	2	3
Mr Cross	Abbots Ltd	4	5
6	7	8	9

Dialogue 1

Adler Well, Mr Sharp, you seem to have a well-organized business here.

Manager I think so, but then we've been in business for over fifteen years in this area.

Adler How big is the company?

Manager In York, there are over thirty vehicles.

Adler They're all recent models, I suppose?

Manager Oh yes, we change models every year.

Adler What are the hire arrangements at Rentex?

Manager There are daily or weekly rates, inclusive of insurance.

Adler What kind of discount do you give?

Manager That depends. There are special rates if the volume is high.

Adler Let me tell you the situation. We're planning to have small tour groups here from May through September. Two days a week they'll need cars.

Manager That shouldn't be a problem.

Adler Right. I'd need the cars delivered to their hotel and collected the following evening.

Manager I see. How many cars are we talking about?

Adler It should be a minimum of five.

Manager All right. Let's look at this in more detail ...

Dialogue 2

Manager ... and this is one of our fifty-three seaters.

Adler Do you have anything smaller than this, Mr Cross?

Manager Yes. There are also thirty-nine and twenty-five seaters.

Adler They say that Abbots are the specialists in local tours.

Manager I think you could say that. There's no other operator that offers the variety that we do.

Adler What sorts of trips are available?

Manager Here's our advertised programme.

Adler Let me see. Yes. Abbeys, castles, the coast. This seems the kind of thing.

Manager And we also arrange special routes and programmes for a customer if there is a demand.

Adler Right. The type of tour I might need is one full day a week during the summer. A thirty-nine seater should do it.

Manager Did you have anything particular in mind?

Adler Well, I've been considering a trip to Castle Howard in the morning, lunch at a country hotel, and some sightseeing in the afternoon.

Manager Fine. Let me get a map and I'll show you ...

Dialogue 3

Secretary Good morning. Ross Travel.

Adler Mr Mason, please.

Secretary Hold the line.

Manager Mason speaking.

Adler This is Dan Adler of Travel International.

Manager Oh, hello Mr Adler. How can I help you?

Adler I'm looking for a handling agent to deal with some transfers on a package we might put together.

Manager I'm sure we can help. What's the situation exactly?

Adler We should have two groups coming into Manchester Airport weekly from May through September. They'll need transfers between the airport and the Crown Hotel.

Manager Good. I've got that. Let me do some checking and I'll get back to you.

Adler OK. You can ring me at the Crown.

Manager Fine. It won't take long.

Study the following examples.

Guest When does the next London flight arrive? (in about ten minutes)
Receptionist *It **should arrive** in about ten minutes.*

Guest When will Mr Samuels be back? (at ten o'clock)
Receptionist *He **should be** back at ten o'clock.*

Now do the exercise on the tape, replying as the Receptionist in a similar way.

Activities

Activity A

Study the following itinerary. It shows the activities and timetable during the first two and a half days of a familiarization tour. The activities for each of the days have been written in the wrong order. Decide the time when each activity should take place.

Day 1 Thursday 8 May

07.20	(1) Inaugural dinner at hotel
10.30	(2) Free time for relaxation
Afternoon	(3) Welcome Cocktail Party with the Director of YHTB
19.30	(4) Arrive Manchester Airport. Transfer by coach
20.00	(5) Check into Grand Spa Hotel, Harrogate

Day 2 Friday 9 May

08.30	(1) View castle. Coffee with its owner
09.30	(2) Reception – Courtesy of Grand Spa Hotel
10.00	(3) Lunch at Old Swan Hotel, Market Square, Ripon
12.30	(4) Optional visit to night club
Afternoon	(5) Return to Grand Spa Hotel
17.30	(6) Full English Breakfast
19.00	(7) Depart by coach deep into Yorkshire Dales on scenic route to Ripley Castle
20.00	(8) Still deeper into the country to visit Grassington and Yorkshire Dales farms
22.30	(9) Gala dinner at the Hotel

Day 3 Saturday 10 May

09.00	(1) Lunch at Matthew's Wine Bar
10.00	(2) Meet York Guides for walking tour of city
11.00	(3) Full English Breakfast
13.00	(4) Depart hotel and drive to York
14.00	(5) Own time free for shopping

Activity B

Place the appropriate word or expression from the list below in the following holiday information list.

a. *Farmhouse*
b. *Walking Holidays*
c. *Study and Leisure*
d. *courses*
e. *Central Heating*
f. *Car Tours*
g. *Cycling Tours*

h. *Bed and breakfast*
i. *experienced guides*
j. *Horse Riding*
k. *instruction*
l. *first-class*
m. *Family Activity Holidays*

SELF-CATERING COTTAGES – Our carefully modernized cottages are situated in attractive villages 10–15 miles from York. __1__ , colour TV, electricity and linen are included in the price. Mrs J Poppleton, 26 Bryant Way, York YO1 2LG. Tel. 0904-21437

__2__ – Explore the natural beauty of the Yorkshire Dales on foot in the company of __3__ . Accommodation and meals are provided in traditional country pubs. Holidays are available from April to October. J Gower, Ramblers Ltd, 30 Terrace Row, Ripon, N. Yorks. Tel. 0765-85213

__4__ – Discover the beautiful countryside on routes chosen to suit all types of cyclist. __5__ accommodation, routes and maps are included in the price. Machines can also be hired. Mrs Grace, 17 Front Street, York YO3 3JL. Tel. 0904-61242

__6__ – Holidays include full board __7__ accommodation and full __8__ (including jumping) by experienced trainers. Suitable for beginners. Colonel Pope, High Ridge Farm, Skipton, West Yorkshire

__9__ – A choice of ten different activities to suit all ages: riding, cycling, fishing and many more. Accommodation in traditional cottages. Activity Centre, Hawes, West Yorkshire

__10__ – In the morning learn English in a well-equipped school. In the afternoon and evening enjoy the extensive holiday programme of visits, lectures, discussions, sport and films. Accommodation is with a family. Two week __11__ from May to September. Marjory Hughes, Inter-Group, 5 Portman Way, York. Tel. 0904-21124

__12__ – 4 day chauffeur-driven tours departing from York for four persons. The itinerary includes visits to the Dales, the Moors, castles, abbeys and the coast. The price of the tour is fully inclusive with __13__ hotel accommodation. L Friel, Carew Ltd, Beech House, Harrogate, N. Yorks. Tel. 0423-6672

Writing

Notice how the following pairs of sentences are linked using **although**, **because**, and **unless.**

Examples:

York is only two hours by train from London. It's over 300 kilometres away.

▶ York is only two hours by train from London **although** it's over 300 kilometres away

We will have to use Manchester Airport. No other airport in the region can take wide-bodied jets.
▶ We shall have to use Manchester Airport **because** no other airport in the region can take wide-bodied jets.

You shouldn't start to prepare a package. You have reached agreement with a carrier.
▶ You shouldn't start to prepare a package **unless** you have reached agreement with a carrier.

Now link the following pairs of sentences using **unless**, **although**, or **because** where appropriate.

1 Most of the tour operators felt the FAM was valuable. It gave them a good idea of the region's tourist potential.
2 The handling agent will deal with the transfers. You prefer to make the arrangements yourself.
3 Gunnar Andersson of Swedtour didn't join the group. He said he was coming.
4 The idea of using the Crown Hotel was rejected. Its manager couldn't accept the operator's offer.
5 Companies providing local facilities don't usually offer discounts. The operator can guarantee quite a large volume of business.
6 Complimentary rooms are normally offered to couriers. There is usually a minimum group size needed for this.
7 A surcharge will be necessary from 1 July. The value of the pound falls.
8 The tour operator made a detailed inspection of the hotel. He had to select suitable accommodation for a FIT.

Word study

activity holidays p. 124, holidays offering special activities such as walking or cycling.
chat p. 125, informal talk.
chef p. 125, cook who works in a large kitchen.
complimentary p. 131, free.
cottage p. 130, small house in the country.
courier p. 131, tour leader.
enclosing p. 124, putting with the letter. *n* **enclosure.**
escorted tours p. 124, tours accompanied by a courier.
familiarization tour p. 129, tour arranged for tour operators so that they can inspect a region and its facilities.
family-oriented p. 124, directed towards families.

fifty-three seater p. 128, coach with fifty-three seats.
gala p. 129, special; festive.
get back to you p. 128, contact you again.
hold the line p. 128, wait.
in association with p. 124, together with.
in the meantime p. 124, before that time; meanwhile.
inaugural p. 129, opening.
independent tours p. 124, tours including flights and hotel only.
insurance p. 128, protection against accidents, loss or damage. *v* **insure.**
itinerary p. 124, travel programme.
leisure p. 130, free time.
linen p. 130, sheets, towels, etc.
lounge bars p. 125, bars with comfortable seating.

low budget p. 124, low cost.

optional visit p. 129, visit that can be made if desired.

participate p. 124, take part. A person who takes part is a **participant.**

proposed p. 124, suggested in a formal way. *n* **proposal.**

pubs p. 132

rack rate p. 127, individual rate for a hotel room.

reception p. 129, welcome party.

scenic route p. 129, route through beautiful countryside.

self-catering arrangements p. 124, arrangements where guests provide and prepare their own food.

suites p. 125, hotel bedrooms with adjoining living rooms.

surcharge p. 131, additional charge.

tourist potential p. 131, possibilities for increasing tourism.

wide-bodied jets p. 131, Tristar, 747, DC 10, Airbus, etc.

A typical English pub.

Unit 11
Tour operation – Negotiation

Reading and Listening

Here is a summary of a report that Jim Gleason of Texas Travel has made to his company.

Subject   Yorkshire FAM

1 Introduction

Earlier this year, UK Airways made a proposal of costings and
schedulings, flying Houston-Manchester UK. The quotes certainly
gave a clear advantage over other carriers, and were guaranteed
through the end of '83.

After I had received this favourable offer, I agreed to a
familiarization tour of the Yorkshire region at the invitation
of their Tourist Board.

2 Recommendation

I am now in a position to report on that tour. My recommendation
is that Texas Travel incorporate a Yorkshire element in their '83
program. I suggest Yorkshire is presented as part of a joint-destination
product - for example, a Yorkshire/Scottish Tour or a Herriot Country/
Shakespeare Country Tour. Such tours would be ideal for a ten-day
FIT.

3 Proposed Arrangements

   a Transfer

   The transfer between airport/hotel/airport would be handled by
   J Parkin & Sons Ltd. This is a well-established firm which has
   put in a very attractive tender for the handling arrangements.

   b Hotel

   The White Rose Hotel, a traditional, well-sited, comfortable
   establishment, has offered very competitive five-day terms
   with full American Plan.

   c Excursions

   Northern Coaches have proposed a tailored program of whole-day
   and half-day excursions which combine the best that the region
   has to offer - city, countryside, and places of interest.

Finally, if Texas Travel is going to sell this destination, we must begin
our detailed preparations within the next month in order to finalize
the brochure.

1 Why did Jim Gleason agree to go on a FAM of Yorkshire?
2 What type of tour programme does Jim Gleason recommend?
3 What type of company is J Parkin & Son Ltd?
4 How many days does Jim Gleason suggest for the Yorkshire part of the package?
5 Why must a decision about the Yorkshire tour be made quickly?

Listening

Listen to the following conversation between Jan Berg, a tour operator from Stockholm, and Bill Wentworth, manager of the Windsor Restaurant in York.

Berg Sorry I'm late, Mr Wentworth. I had hoped to be here earlier, but I was held up.

Wentworth That's quite all right, Mr Berg. No problem. Now, you wanted to talk about dinner arrangements for some groups, I believe.

Berg That's right. My groups are going to be in York for two nights. I'd like them to have a traditional Yorkshire dinner on the second night. You do that sort of meal, don't you?

Wentworth We certainly do, as a fully inclusive arrangement.

Berg Exactly what is included?

Wentworth Well, there's the traditional meal itself: four courses, drinks before and during the meal, after-dinner coffee, and service.

Berg That seems clear enough, apart from the drinks. What do they get?

Wentworth A sherry before the meal and a glass of red wine during it.

Berg What about white wine for those that prefer it?

Wentworth Oh yes. But as the main course is roast beef most people prefer to drink the red.

Berg They'll probably want to drink more than one glass.

Wentworth In that case, they can order it by the glass, carafe or bottle. And our prices there are very competitive.

Berg Are you providing entertainment? Swedish restaurants often have a dance floor.

Wentworth We have a three-piece band playing every night during the season, and there's a small dance floor. The music isn't too loud or fast.

Listening check

1 How long are the tour groups going to stay in York?
2 What kind of meal does Mr Berg want to arrange for the groups?
3 What is included in the set meal?
4 Why do most people prefer red wine with this meal?
5 What kind of entertainment will be provided?

Language study

Past time

Notice how we can use the Past Perfect to combine sentences.

Example:

First, I received a favourable price from the carrier. Then I accepted the invitation to a FAM. (after)

▶ After I **had received** a favourable price from the carrier, I accepted the invitation to a FAM.

Now combine the following pairs of sentences in a similar way.

1 I made an inspection of the hotel facilities. Following that, I made a report to the Managing Director. (after)
2 First, the group attended a reception at the Globe Hotel. After that, they had a guided tour of the city. (after)
3 The tour operator agreed the '83 group rates with the Falcon Hotel. Before that, the tour operator visited five hotels in the region. (before)
4 The journalists arrived at Hull. They then travelled directly to Harrogate by coach. (after)
5 Texas Travel included the Grand Hotel in their '83 bed plan. Before that, their representative inspected the hotel. (before)

Future time

Study the following 'Action Pad' of a tour operator.

action	comment
1 Meet UK Airways rep.	arranged for 24 March
2 Inspect Globe Hotel facilities	maybe next week
3 Check sales plan	intended for week after next
4 Report to Managing Director	appointment 9 am Tuesday next
5 Propose changes to '83 program	preferably at next management meeting
6 Go on FAM of Morocco	possibly June or July
7 Visit advertising agency	scheduled for 2 June
8 Write UK report	tomorrow, if there is time
9 Sign contract with Arrow Hotels	as soon as possible
10 Take a day off	next Friday, definitely

Notice how we use the Present Continuous Tense to express individual plans and arrangements for the future, the 'Going to' form to express intention, and the Simple Future to express uncertainty.

I am meeting the UK Airways representative on 24 March.
Perhaps **I'll inspect** the facilities at the Globe Hotel next week.
I am going to check the sales plan the week after next.

Now write appropriate sentences for 4–10.

Reporting questions

Notice how we report the two types of question.

'Are all the rooms air-conditioned?' (He asked)
He asked **whether/if** all the rooms **were** air-conditioned.
'When do they have to sign the agreement?' (She wondered)
She wondered **when** they **had** to sign the agreement.

Now report the following questions in a similar way.

1 'Will the trade fair be in February or March?' (He wanted to know)
2 'Why hasn't the carrier confirmed the flight costings?' (He asked)

3 'When is the New York flight due?' (She wanted to know)
4 'Can the handling agent arrange the tour?' (He wondered)
5 'How long has Mr Pinar been staying?' (They inquired)
6 'Does that rate include all taxes?' (She asked me)
7 'Where will the meeting take place?' (He wanted to know)
8 'Is there a supplement payable on single rooms?' (He inquired)

Listening and Speaking

Listening

Mr Stephen Altman, a tour operator, is discussing tour arrangements with Frank Gerard, the General Manager of the Carlton Hotel. While you are listening to their conversation, complete the table below.

proposed tour details	
Tour season	1
Duration of tour	2
Specified days	3
Number per tour (low season)	4
Number per tour (high season)	5
Financial guarantees offered	6
Length of release-back clause	7

Gerard Have you enjoyed your look over the hotel?

Altman Just fine. Now what about us talking a little more in detail about possible arrangements?

Gerard By all means. First, what about a drink of some sort? Gin, whisky, Martini?

Altman I'll take a gin and tonic, please.

Gerard Certainly. ... Right. Here you are.

Altman Thank you. Cheers.

Gerard Let me see. Here's our normal tariff. Take a look.

Altman OK. These are all rack rates. Right?

Gerard That's right.

Altman What's the position on groups?

Gerard Well, there are a number of factors to consider. First, how big are the groups going to be? Second, what time of the year are they going to come, and, for that matter, which part of the week?

Altman And I guess you're interested in American Plan or modified American Plan.

Gerard Of course. If you only want Continental Plan then the hotel gets used less, and there's less in it for us.

Altman Well, there are different ways we could approach this. We could look at the total demand for accommodation over the year and fix a price, or maybe negotiate a number of different prices according to the time of year.

Gerard Of course, but let's take one step at a time. What kind of numbers are we talking about?

Altman Well. We're going to sell the tour April through October. We would hope for forty-five people weekly in the earlier part of the season, doubling that figure during the high season, then falling back to forty-five again.

Gerard And for how many nights?

Altman That's four nights.

Gerard Is that mid-week? Weekends?

Altman To take advantage of our flight arrangements, it would be Friday through Tuesday.

Gerard I see. Tell me, what kind of guarantees are you offering on the arrangements?

Altman We're not prepared to make any guarantees at all.

Gerard None at all? No deposits?

Altman No. No money up front at all.

Gerard That's rather a lot to ask of any hotelier.

Altman Come on, Mr Gerard. This is not unusual. And you are dealing with a company with a good name that usually sells what it targets.

Gerard I accept that. But don't you see the risks involved?

Altman We're in business. Besides, there would be a three-month release-back clause in the contract.

Gerard I don't know. I mean, ninety beds during all the high season weekends. That's a lot.

Altman Yes. And so is forty-five in May and September.

Gerard Certainly. But I have to think of my regular trade.

Altman It's beginning to look as if you're not too interested in doing business.

Gerard No, no. I didn't say that. It's just that not long after the hotel had opened we had a rather bad experience with this kind of block booking.

Altman It depends who you are dealing with, Mr Gerard. Let me put it this way. For the kind of business we have in mind, I think an average discount in the region of 15 to 20% is ...

<table>
<tr><td>

Speaking

Confirming
information

</td><td>

Notice in the two examples below how question tags are used with a falling tone in order to confirm information.

</td></tr>
</table>

Service isn't included.
Tour operator *Service isn't included, is it?*

The guests can order extra wine.
Tour operator *The guests can order extra wine, can't they?*

Now do the exercise on the tape, adding question tags in a similar way to confirm the information given.

Activities

<table>
<tr><td>

Activity A

</td><td>

Two tour operators have been negotiating with an hotel chain. The tour operators have each agreed to a different kind of deal.

</td></tr>
</table>

Tour Operator A

Tour Operator A has been offered a 20% discount per person based on the rack rate of £29. The operator must take the following amount of accommodation:

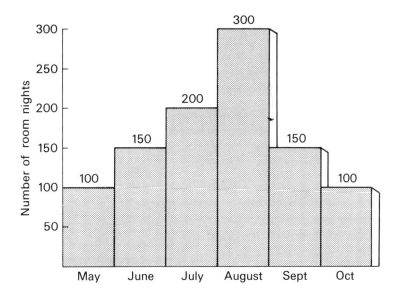

Tour Operator B

Tour Operator B has been offered different rates depending on the total amount booked. For example, if only 300 room nights are booked, they are charged at £27:

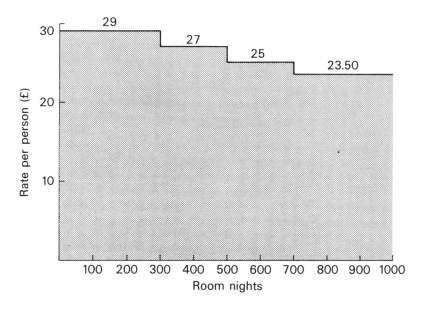

If all the room nights on offer are taken, who has the better deal: Tour Operator A or Tour Operator B?

Study the Paris–London rail/ship/hovercraft timetable and the London–York rail timetable.

Paris-London

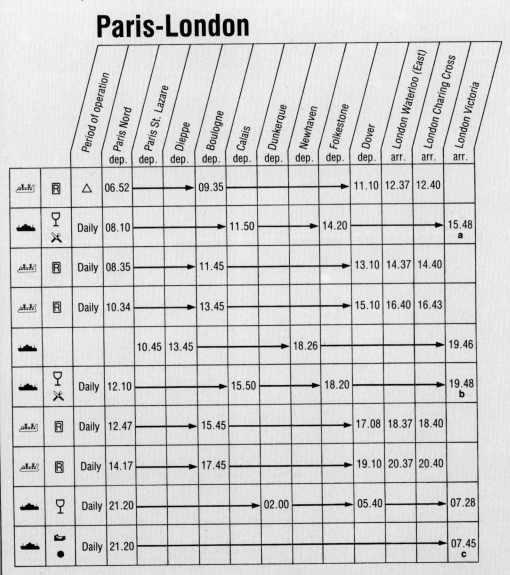

		Period of operation	Paris Nord dep.	Paris St. Lazare dep.	Dieppe dep.	Boulogne dep.	Calais dep.	Dunkerque dep.	Newhaven dep.	Folkestone dep.	Dover dep.	London Waterloo (East) arr.	London Charing Cross arr.	London Victoria arr.
hovercraft	R	△	06.52				09.35					11.10	12.37	12.40	
ship	♀ ✕	Daily	08.10					11.50			14.20				15.48 a
hovercraft	R	Daily	08.35				11.45					13.10	14.37	14.40	
hovercraft	R	Daily	10.34				13.45					15.10	16.40	16.43	
ship				10.45	13.45					18.26					19.46
ship	♀ ✕	Daily	12.10					15.50			18.20				19.48 b
hovercraft	R	Daily	12.47				15.45					17.08	18.37	18.40	
hovercraft	R	Daily	14.17				17.45					19.10	20.37	20.40	
ship	♀	Daily	21.20						02.00			05.40			07.28
ship	🛏 ●	Daily	21.20												07.45 c

🚢	Sealink Ship with on-board catering.		△	Mondays to Fridays 29 September to 24 October
🚁	Seaspeed hovercraft.		●	Night Ferry. 1st Class only
🛏	Sleeper service.		a	Saturdays arr. 15.59, Sundays arr. 16.07
♀	Buffet service London-Dover/Folkestone.		b	Saturdays and Sundays arr. 20.07
✕	Buffet car or Tray meal service Calais-Paris.		c	Saturdays arr. 08.00.
R	Reservations compulsory.			

London King's Cross ⟶ Selby ⟶ York

King's Cross dep.	Selby *FP* arr.	York *P* arr.		Notes	
00.02	03.41	04.00		A	Sleeping car passengers only
01.10	06.52 d	07.11 d		B	Mondays excepted
05.50	08.37	08.55		E	Not 30 May
125 ■ 07.32 ✗①	⟶	09.52		F	Fridays only
125 ■ 08.00 ✗①	10.37 d	10.19		G	23 May
125 09.00 ✗①	⟶	11.16		K	Holders of other than Awayday tickets
125 09.35 ①	⟶	11.45			can arrive King's Cross at 09.25
10.05 ⚏	12.48	13.06		M	Mondays only
125 11.00 ✗①	⟶	13.11		N	By changing at Doncaster passengers
125 11.35 ✗①	13.43 d	13.45			can arrive King's Cross 01.51
12.20 ✗⚏	14.51	15.10			
125 13.00 ✗①	⟶	15.15		d	Change at Doncaster
125 13.35 ①	16.21 d	15.51		*FP*	Free parking at or near station
14.05 ⚏	16.46	17.04		*P*	Car parking at station—fee payable
125 15.00 ✗①	⟶	17.08		■	Accommodation may be limited
125 15.35 ✗①	17.44 d	17.45			All seats reservable
16.05 ⚏	18.46	19.04			
125 16.40 ✗①	⟶	18.53			
125 ■ 17.00 ✗①	⟶	19.11			
125 17.35 ✗①	⟶	19.44			
18.05 ⚏	20.41	21.01		Information is subject to alteration,	
125 19.00 ✗①	22.41 d	21.12		especially at Public Holidays	
125 F 19.53 ①	22.41 d	22.13			
20.00	⟶	23.11			
20.15	⟶	23.59			
22.30	⟶	01.51			

Decide on the travel arrangements for the following clients who wish to travel from Paris to York. Indicate where reservations are necessary or advisable.

The transfer time between London Charing Cross or London Victoria and London King's Cross is 45 minutes.

1 M Beauvoir has to be in York by 11.30 on Monday. He wishes to travel first class.
2 The Levasseur family want to leave Paris on Thursday morning and arrive in York early the same evening. They don't like travelling by hovercraft.
3 Mme Hamadi would like to be in York by 15.00 on Saturday afternoon. She is travelling second class.
4 Peter Johnson wants to travel to London on Tuesday. Any departure time is suitable but the journey must be as short as possible. He would like to travel to York as early as possible on Wednesday morning and have breakfast on the train.

Writing

Here is the main part of a letter from a tour operator to an hotelier. It confirms various points that were discussed at a meeting the previous week.

Dear Mr Morse,

re Hotel Arrangements for Starways Ltd

I would like to confirm in writing the arrangements that we agreed last week for the 1983 program.

1 Schedule

A From 13 May through 16 July, 33 bed nights every Friday and Saturday. Guests will arrive at 18.00 on Friday and depart 10.00 on Sunday.

B From 22 July through 30 August, 66 bed nights every Friday and Saturday, and every Monday and Tuesday.

2 Accommodation

For Period A above, we will require 12 twin-bedded rooms with shower, and 9 single rooms with shower. For Period B above, we will require 24 twin-bedded rooms with shower, and 18 single rooms with shower.

The groups will require full American Plan with an additional packed lunch on the day of departure.

3 Release-back

We agreed that a two-month release-back clause would operate.

I hope this represents the discussions we had. I would be grateful if you would let me know if you have any further comments. Meanwhile, I will have a contract drawn up.

Yours sincerely,

Frank Schultz
General Manager

Now write similar letters confirming the following details that were agreed at various meetings.

1 From: Mr Leonard Bellman, a tour operator
   To: Mr Gerald Rossiter, the proprietor of a local tour firm
   Subject: Full-day tour program for '83

   a. Full-day tour of Yorkshire Dales – to include stops at Reeth,
      Hawes, and Grassington
   b. Every Thursday morning 6 May through 11 September inclusive
   c. 1 35-seater bus. Pick up 09.15 Lawton Hotel, York/Set down
      approx. 16.30 at Lawton Hotel.

2 From: Mr Drew Masters, a tour operator
   To: Mr Arnold Stevens, an hotelier
   Subject: Hotel arrangements for '83

   a. 56 people for 3 nights every Monday, Tuesday, Wednesday
      weekly 2 May through 17 September. Arrive 17.00 Monday/
      Depart 09.00 Thursday.
   b. Require 20 twins with showers/16 singles with showers. Full
      American Plan.
   c. Option on 20 further twins for period 30 July–17 September.

3 From: Mrs Wilma Stanton, a tour operator
   To: Mr Clive Denton, a handling agent
   Subject: Transfer arrangements for '83

   a. Every Tuesday, 1 May–16 September, pick up 59 passengers at
      Manchester Airport off UK 672 Houston–Manchester. Arriving
      11.25. Transfer to Grand Hotel, York
   b. Every Thursday, 10 May–25 September, pick up 59 passengers at
      Grand Hotel, York. Transfer to Manchester Airport for UK 312
      Manchester–Paris CDG. Departing 09.50

Word study

advertising agency p. 136, company
  which prepares advertisements.
American Plan p. 137, full board.
  Modified American Plan is room,
  breakfast and dinner.
apart from p. 135, except.
appointment p. 136, time arranged
  for a meeting.
based on p. 138, calculated on.
bed plan p. 136, plan used by a tour
  operator which describes the flight
  arrangements and hotel
  arrangements for tour groups.
block booking p. 138, booking of a
  number of beds at one time.

compulsory p. 140, necessary;
  obligatory.
Continental Plan p. 137, bed and
  breakfast. **European Plan** is bed
  only.
contract p. 136, formal agreement,
  usually written.
drawn up p. 142, prepared.
excursions p. 134, local tours.
favourable p. 134, advantageous.
fix a price p. 137, decide on a price.
ideal p. 134, perfect.
in the region of p. 138, about;
  aproximately.
incorporate p. 134, include.

joint-destination p. 134, combination of two destinations.

packed lunch p. 142, picnic lunch.

proprietor p. 142, owner.

quotes p. 134, prices offered by a supplier. The full form is **quotations**. *v* **quote**.

release-back clause p. 137, clause in a contract between a tour operator and an hotelier which provides for a period of notice, eg two months, if the tour operator does not need the beds he has booked.

risks p. 138, dangers.

supplement p. 137, additional cost.

tailored p. 134, specially prepared.

targets p. 138, aims, objectives.

tender p. 134, price offered by a supplier, usually in writing.

three-piece band p. 135, group of three musicians.

up front p. 138, in advance.

well-sited p. 134, in a good position.

Unit 12
Conferences

Reading and Listening

This information is taken from the Meeting Guide to Hong Kong prepared by the Hong Kong Tourist Association.

Hong Kong Tourist Association
London Office
香港旅遊協會倫敦辦事處

Planning and promoting the meeting in Hong Kong

Once the decision to meet in Hong Kong has been made, the HKTA is happy to advise on all the details connected with organizing and promoting your meeting.

Services include:

* Introductions to professional meeting organizers and display companies.

* Information about, and liaison with, Hong Kong public figures to provide welcome addresses at opening ceremonies and dinner functions.

* Public relations contacts with local TV, press, and trade media.

* Advice on Customs and Immigration procedures to facilitate entry for delegates and speedy clearance for literature and display material.

* Special arrangements for an HKTA representative to attend preceding events in order to assist in promoting Hong Kong as the next destination with supplies of appropriate literature and display material, films, and audio visual presentation.

* Providing supplies of promotional literature for your mailing to potential delegates. This will assist in generating maximum interest and attendance. Material can be overprinted with the organizer's own text.

* Listing of the event in the Association's calendar, 'Coming Meetings, Conferences and Exhibitions', widely distributed throughout the world and updated biannually.

* Ideas on 'Theme' evenings for gala functions with names of suppliers and costs. A comprehensive list of local entertainment groups and arts and crafts specialists that can be hired for social programmes.

* Details of exciting and educational tours for accompanying persons who are not attending the meeting sessions.

* Arranging for a 'Welcome' banner to be displayed at airport.

1 What 'Welcome' facilities can be arranged?
2 How can the HKTA make it easier for delegates to enter the country?
3 How does the HKTA assist in encouraging maximum attendance at a conference?
4 In which calendar are events listed?
5 Who are educational tours arranged for?

Michael Snow is making enquiries about conference facilities to Wen Tsang, Assistant Manager of the Regent Hotel, Hong Kong. While you are listening to the conversation, refer to the ground plans of the hotel below.

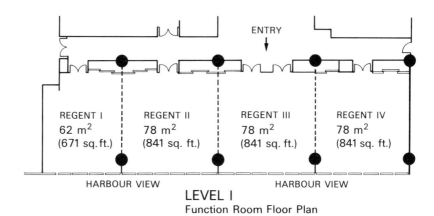

LEVEL I
Function Room Floor Plan

LEVEL II
Function Rooms Floor Plan

Tsang This is Mr Tsang speaking.

Snow Hello, this is Michael Snow of the Lawn Medical Foundation. Would you mind giving me some information on the Regent conference facilities?

Tsang Certainly, Mr Snow. What size of conference do you have in mind?

Snow Well, we will have finalized the numbers by next month. We intend having about 160 delegates.

Tsang I see. What kind of facilities would you need?

Snow We would need both classroom and theatre accommodation.

Tsang Let me give you two possibilities. We have our Regent Function Rooms One to Four which are all interconnected. These provide over two thousand square feet. Or we have Regent Five and Six, also interconnected, which give about seventeen hundred square feet.

Snow I see. And what is the capacity of these two areas?

Tsang Regent One to Four seat one hundred and eighty people when used as classrooms or three hundred and ten when used as a theatre. Regent Five and Six hold one hundred and sixty as classrooms and two hundred as a theatre.

Snow Right. I've got that. Now what about office support services?

Tsang We have telex, photocopying, secretarial services, and also a photographer if required.

Snow And the technical equipment for the classrooms?

Tsang We are fully equipped. There are movie, slide, and overhead projectors.

Snow How about basic equipment such as tape recorders, easel pads, markers, microphones, loudspeakers, that sort of thing?

Tsang Yes, they're provided.

Snow Right. That seems fine. I don't think there's anything else.

Tsang Well, Mr Snow, if you give me your address I can send . . . .

Listening check

1 Approximately how many delegates are expected at the Lawn Medical Foundation Conference?
2 What is the total area of Regent Function Rooms 1–4?
3 What is the capacity of Regent Function Rooms 5 and 6 if they are used as a theatre?
4 What office support services are provided by the Regent Hotel?
5 What kind of projection equipment is available?

Language study

Future time

Notice how we can use the Future Perfect to talk about events that will be complete at some time in the future.

They are introducing a 10% surcharge on all bills. This will happen before next week.
▶ They **will have introduced** a 10% surcharge on all bills before next week.

Now combine the sentences below in a similar way.

1 International Hotels Inc are building their new conference centre. It will be ready by the end of the year.
2 The committee are finishing the preparations for the group. They will be finalized very soon.
3 The housekeeping staff are cleaning those rooms. They will be ready in an hour.
4 All the delegates are receiving this information. They will have it at least a month before the conference.
5 The delegates are arriving at the moment. They'll all be here within two or three hours.
6 UK Airways are not introducing new aircraft on this route yet. That won't happen before the late eighties.

Dimensions

Notice how we can talk about the dimensions of a room.

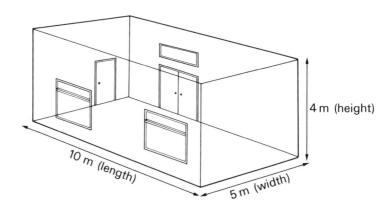

Dimensions of a room

What is the **height/width/length** of the room?
▶ The **height** is 4 metres ...

or How **high/wide/long** is the room?
▶ The room is 4 metres **high** ...

What is the **area** of the room?
▶ The area is 50 **square metres**.

Now write out similar questions and answers about the two rooms below.

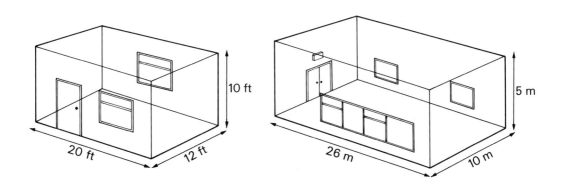

Some verbs can be followed by the Gerund, some by the Infinitive,
and some by either the Gerund or the Infinitive. For example,

Do you mind **giving** me some more details?
I hope **to mail** potential delegates tomorrow.
Do you prefer **travelling** first class?
or Do you prefer **to travel** first class?

There is no easy way of being sure which combination is correct. You
should find out and learn the correct usage. Now find out which form
follows these verbs.

1 I suggest ... the conference in May. (hold)
2 Do you intend ... a preliminary announcement? (send)
3 When will you arrange ... the speakers? (contact)
4 Have you considered ... a post-conference tour? (organize)
5 The delegates hope ... their families with them. (bring)
6 Do you agree ... the meeting venue by 23 June? (confirm)
7 When will you start ... the conference programme? (prepare)
8 The organizers should postpone ... a decision until next
   week. (make)

Listening and Speaking

Listening

Mr Leong, of the Hong Kong Tourist Authority, and Mr Harding, a
member of the International Legal Computing Association, are
discussing conference arrangements in Hong Kong. While you are
listening to their conversation, complete the Conference Enquiry Form
and the Conference Package Breakdown of Costs.

Element	Cost/HK$
6 nights $\frac{1}{2}$ twin room HK\$200 + 14%	a
APT – HTL – APT transfers	b
c	72
3 lunches	d
e	120
f	70
Total Cost	g

Conference package breakdown of costs

CONFERENCE ENQUIRY FORM

1. NATURE OF ENQUIRY & NAME OF EVENT   (✓)

   Exhibition _____   Conference _____   Seminar _____

   Int'l Conf _____   P C Tour _____   Workshop _____

2. NAME & ADDRESS OF ORGANIZATION IN YOUR REGION/MARKET

   International Legal Computing Association, _____

   1430 Tung Ming Building, 40 Des Voeux, C., Hong Kong _____

3. NAME & ADDRESS OF INTERNATIONAL ORGANIZATION (IF APPROPRIATE)

   _____

   _____

   _____

4. PROPOSED DATE & DURATION OF EVENT

   Date : _____   Duration : _____

5. ESTIMATED ATTENDANCE

   Delegates _____   Accompanying Persons _____   Exhibitors _____

   International Delegates _____   Hong Kong Delegates _____

6. BEDROOMS REQUIRED

   Twin _____   Single _____   Suites _____

7. MEETING FACILITIES REQUIRED

   Size _____   Set up: theatre/classroom/round-table (delete where not
                                                                applicable)

   No. of Meeting Rooms _____   No. of Booths/Size _____

   Exhibition Space _____

Harding Good morning, Mr Leong. My name's George Harding. I'm with the International Legal Computing Association. We're starting to prepare next year's conference. We'd like to hold it in Hong Kong so I thought I'd give you a ring to see if you can offer any assistance.

Leong We'd be very glad to help, Mr Harding. When do you intend to hold the conference?

Harding It's due to take place in mid-November next year. We'd like the delegates to arrive in Hong Kong on the 12th or 13th of November as the conference starts on the 14th. It'll last for five days.

Leong I see. Do you mind giving me a few more details? What's the Association's address?

Harding It's 35 Curzon Street, London W1Y 2AC. And the phone number is 01-499-9211.

Leong Good. Is there a branch in Hong Kong?

Harding Yes, in fact there is. The address is 1430 Tung Ming Building, 40 Des Voeux, C., Hong Kong. Phone: 5-242640. The person to contact there is Mr Chung.

Leong Fine. Perhaps you could give me some idea of the size of the conference and the amount of accommodation required?

Harding We would expect about 240 people to attend. Of these, 30 will be from Hong Kong itself. The rest will require hotel accommodation, mainly in twin rooms. 30 singles should be enough. We'll need a meeting room with theatre layout big enough for all the delegates.

Leong What about group rooms?

Harding We'll need five of those, seating up to 40 people each, for workshops. With all the usual AV aids. Those are our basic requirements. Could you give me a rough idea of what an arrangement like this would cost?

Leong Certainly. I can give you the details of a conference package at one of the top international hotels in Hong Kong. The costings are based on 100 twin rooms.

Harding The figures are this year's, I suppose?

Leong Yes, that's right. They're valid until the end of this year. Of course, by next year the costs will have increased. The package comprises six nights' accommodation, including service and tax, transfer from the airport to the hotel and back, five days' meeting-room use, a welcome cocktail reception in our hospitality room, a half-day Hong Kong Island tour and a farewell banquet. The total cost is 1900 Hong Kong dollars, or a little over £160.

Harding That sounds fairly reasonable. Could you give me a breakdown so that I can see what each part of the package costs?

Leong I'd be glad to. The room element is HK$ 200, for half a twin room, plus 14% for tax and service times six. That comes to HK$ 1368 for the accommodation. The welcome reception is HK$ 72. The lunches are HK$ 80 each. The group transfer is by coach and costs HK$ 30. The island tour is HK$ 70. I think that covers everything. Oh no, I've forgotten the farewell banquet. That's another HK$ 120. Have you got all that?

Harding Yes, I think so. That sounds most interesting. I will have discussed this with my management committee by the end of next week. Perhaps I could ring you then.

Leong Fine, Mr Harding. I'll look forward to hearing from you.

Speaking
Giving
dimensions

Study the following examples.

Organizer Could you tell me the floor area of the room? (105m²)
Manager *The area is one hundred and five square metres.*

Organizer What is the length of the ballroom? (125 ft)
Manager *The length is one hundred and twenty five feet.*

Now do the exercise on the tape, giving the dimensions in a similar way, using the information provided.

Organizer What is the total exhibition area?
Manager (4,200 ft²)

Organizer How wide is the meeting-room?
Manager (20 ft)

Organizer What is the ceiling height of the room?
Manager (5 m)

Organizer How long is the conference room?
Manager (33½ m)

Organizer What is the width of the hall?
Manager (11 m)

Activities

Activity A

Study the following information taken from the Hong Kong Tourist Authority's Conference Planning Manual.

> **Preliminary Announcement to Delegates**
>
> Naturally, an extremely important step to take is to inform possible delegates in good time that a conference of interest to them is in the planning stage. A first mailing should be prepared for all likely delegates, using a reliable mailing list.

> **Second Announcement – Delegates**
>
> Following the initial announcement that you are going to hold a conference in Hong Kong, you should follow up with a second more comprehensive announcement to all interested parties, together with a detailed registration form.

Now look at the following list of items of information and documentation. Decide which items should be included in the Preliminary Announcement and which in the Second Announcement.

1 Registration form
2 Conference programme
3 Preliminary dates
4 Cancellation fee information
5 Detailed information on Hong Kong in relevant languages
6 A precise figure for registration fees and additional activities
7 Intended speakers and subjects
8 Confirmation of all information, venues, dates, etc
9 Speakers invited and accepted
10 Details of accompanying persons' programme
11 The proposed registration fee and what it includes
12 Theme or subject of the conference
13 Notice of a late registration penalty
14 An introduction to the sponsors and to Hong Kong

Activity B

When planning a conference it is necessary to be well organized. The following diagram shows the planning stages of the Transport Committee and the Accommodation Committee for a conference. Choose from the list of activities below to complete the diagram.

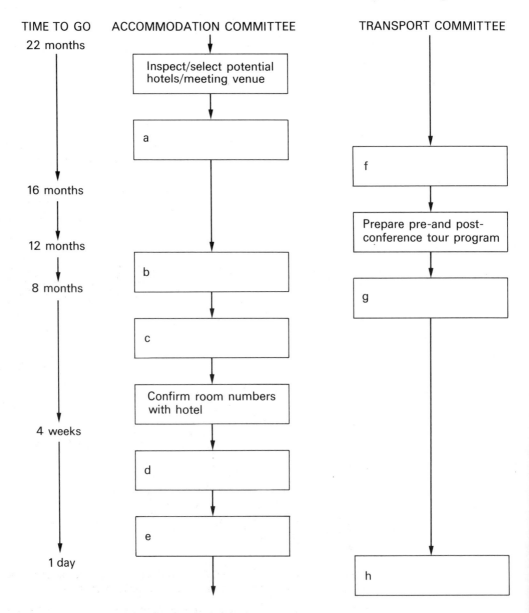

1 Pay hotel deposits
2 Review delegate response
3 Finalize accompanying persons' programme
4 Negotiate and book hotels/meeting venues
5 Select and appoint airlines/tour operators/travel agents
6 Advise hotels of special requirements, eg menus and AV equipment
7 Airport transfer service commences
8 Confirm with hotels function room seating arrangements

Writing

The IASCM (International Association of Shopping Centre Managers) is planning to hold its annual conference at the Ming Garden Hotel in Hong Kong between 8 and 12 November. The manager responsible for organizing the conference, Paul Hennell, often uses the telex. Here is one of the messages he has sent.

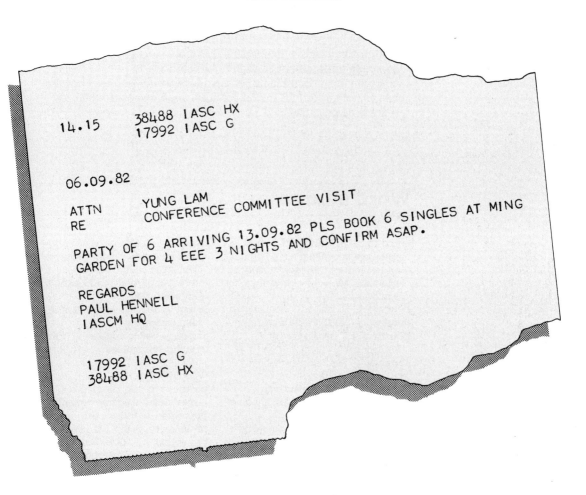

```
14.15        38488 IASC HX
             17992 IASC G


06.09.82

ATTN      YUNG LAM
RE        CONFERENCE COMMITTEE VISIT

PARTY OF 6 ARRIVING 13.09.82 PLS BOOK 6 SINGLES AT MING
GARDEN FOR 4 EEE 3 NIGHTS AND CONFIRM ASAP.

REGARDS
PAUL HENNELL
IASCM HQ

17992 IASC G
38488 IASC HX
```

Using the telex numbers given, now write out the following telex messages. Use appropriate dates and times.

1 ● Yung Lam, at the Hong Kong branch of the IASCM (38488 IASC HX), has confirmed to Paul Hennell that he has booked six single rooms for three nights. He has also urgently requested arrival details for the committee.

● Paul Hennell has replied that they are now only five in number and that they will be arriving on British Airways (BA 3) at 15.15 on Thursday 13 August.

2 • Paul Hennell, at the IASCM HQ in London, has informed Joos Plesman at the Dutch IASCM office (26 449 IASC NL) that the registration period is nearly over. No registrations have been received from the Netherlands. There is a late registration fee that is payable.

   • Joos Plesman has replied apologizing for the delay and requesting the rapid registration of three delegates and two accompanying persons.

3 • Paul Hennell has confirmed to the Ming Garden Hotel that the IASCM will require the 160 twin rooms and 45 singles he had previously booked, plus an extra 20 twin rooms.

   • The Ming Garden has replied that it only has 165 twin rooms available during that period but that there are 15 double rooms that could be used. There is no problem with the 45 singles. The hotel has asked Mr Hennell to contact them about the 15 doubles as quickly as possible.

Word study

audio visual presentation p. 146, presentation making use of sight and sound, eg with tape recordings and films. **AV** is the abbreviation for audio visual.

banquet p. 152, large, formal dinner.

biannually p. 146, twice a year.

branch p. 152, local office of a company.

capacity p. 148, number that can be accommodated.

Customs p. 146, government department which checks imports and exports.

delegates p. 146, people attending a conference.

documentation p. 153, documents, ie pieces of written information.

exhibitions p. 146, public displays of, for example, products and pictures.

facilitate p. 146, make easier.

function room p. 148, room used for meetings, lectures, dinners, etc.

generating p. 146, producing.

hospitality room p. 152, room used for the reception and entertainment of guests.

Immigration p. 146, government department that deals with the entry of people into a country.

initial p. 153, first.

interconnected p. 148, connected with each other.

interested parties p. 153, people who are interested.

layout p. 152, arrangement of seating and equipment.

liaison p. 146, co-operation. v **liaise**.

opening ceremonies p. 146, formal occasions at the opening of conferences.

postpone p. 150, delay until a later date; defer. n **postponement**.

preceding p. 146, earlier.

preliminary p. 153, introductory.

promoting p. 146, encouraging the success of. n **promotion**.

public figures p. 146, well-known people.

relevant p. 153, appropriate.

rough idea p. 152, approximate idea.

sponsors p. 153, organization or company which pays for an event. v **sponsor**.

theme p. 146, central idea.

trade media p. 146, newspapers and magazines connected with the trade.

valid p. 152, in operation; applicable.

venue p. 153 , meeting place.

Revision Unit 3

The exercises in this unit are revision of some of the work studied in units 9–12 of this course.

1 Verbs + prepositions

Complete the sentences below with appropriate prepositions.

1 Our costings are based ... last year's prices plus 15%.
2 Accompanying persons don't participate ... the conference meetings.
3 The HKTA will be glad to assist ... organizing the meeting.
4 The hotel's conference rooms are equipped ... all the necessary AV aids.
5 Very few of the delegates were accompanied ... their wives.
6 The carrier's representative didn't really agree ... us on that point.
7 The Association's international department liaises ... the foreign branches.
8 The interest in optional tours depends, to some extent, ... the weather.

2 Vocabulary

Choose the correct word from those in brackets to complete the following sentences.

1 The tour group had to pay a (service charge/surcharge/charge) because of the increase in fuel costs.
2 The (visitor/occupancy/accommodation) level at the Grand Hotel was 92% during the summer.
3 The conference package included an (optional/accompanying/initial) banquet on the final day.
4 The FAM was (sponsored/quoted/tendered) by the English Tourist Board.
5 After negotiating, the tour operator drew up a (documentation/contract/clause) with the hotelier.
6 Hong Kong was chosen as the (venue/meeting/function) for the medical conference.
7 The organizers made a (previous/preceding/preliminary) announcement in order to inform members of the next annual conference.
8 Your train ticket is (guaranteed/secured/valid) for three months.

3 Comprehension

Study the timetable on the next page. It gives information about Skybus flights to the Caribbean during the 1981 season. Then answer the questions below.

1 Do all passengers have a 20 kg. baggage allowance?
2 What does IRC stand for?
3 What is the price for a thirteen year old accompanied child travelling in August on a ticket booked early in July?
4 Which tax is not included in the price?
5 How long does the flight from London (Luton Airport) to St. Lucia take before 24 October?
6 How much did a man who travelled from Luton on 16 November pay? He booked his ticket on 11 November and had nine kilos of excess baggage.
7 What is provided free during flights?
8 How much did a family of five that left Luton on 23 July pay? The ages of the children were 1, 7 and 14. The booking was made in June.

Caribbean

WEEKLY DEPARTURES EVERY SATURDAY FROM 02 MAY TO 28 NOVEMBER 1981 FROM LONDON TO ST. LUCIA – 7 NIGHTS DURATION, EXTENDABLE TO MAXIMUM 56 NIGHTS

Flight information all times are local

Saturday OM 503	Departure day Flight no.	Saturday OM 504
11.00 16.30	Luton St. Lucia	08.00* 18.30

*following day
Time difference from London until 24 October, – 5 hours, from 25 October, – 4 hours

Prices

BARGAIN* 02 May to 28 November	SALE 02 May to 15 July	STANDARD 16 July to 28 November
£275	£295	£345

*BARGAIN bookable *only during the last 7 days prior to departure*

Your price includes
● Return jet flight ● Baggage allowance of 20 kilos *(44 pounds)* including hand luggage per passenger *(except infants 0-2 years)* ● Meals during flights ● Free wine with main meals during flights ● Complimentary bar service during flights ● The service of a Pegasus courier during flights ● Accommodation throughout your stay (for which a nominal charge of £1 per person is made) ● UK airport taxes and security charges ● All International Route Charges (IRC) ● Delayed departure insurance

It does not include
● Transport to/from UK and Caribbean airports ● Travel insurance ● Food, drink or any personal expenses ● Airport tax on departure from the Caribbean (approx. £2) ● Excess baggage (over 20 kilos) charges of £4 per kilo per sector (or EC$25)

Children's discount
Valid for all prices quoted (available only to children travelling with at least one parent or other adult member of the family).

● Infants up to 2 years	FREE
● Children from 2 to 12 years	30% discount
● Children from 12 to 16 years	20% discount

No limit to the number of children travelling at discount rates!

---

4 Verb tenses and forms

In the following sentences, place the word(s) in brackets in the correct tense and/or form.

1 The Ming Garden Hotel ... last year by a public figure. (open)
2 Long-haul visitors ... less frequently, but spend more. (come)
3 What would happen if there ... another increase in the price of fuel? (be)
4 They ... all the preparations by the time the delegates arrive. (not finish)
5 Mr Suarez is still at the hotel. He ... since the beginning of last week. (stay)
6 The morning flight to Tunis ... at 10.15 (leave)

7 After the group ... from the airport, they attended a reception in the hospitality suite. (arrive)
8 If a hotel ... a high occupancy rate, it is not likely to find group rates very attractive. (have)
9 Have you considered ... a different carrier? (use)
10 Conferences ... at the hotel since the early sixties. (not hold)

5 Multiple choice

Complete the following sentences in an appropriate way.

1 The most important element of a tour operator's preparations is to
   a. arrange interesting local tours
   b. have a favourable agreement with a carrier
   c. establish good relations with hoteliers
   d. appoint a good handling agent

2 An example of a promotional fare is a
   a. standby
   b. FIT
   c. return ticket

3 Low budget package tour arrangements often include
   a. courier service
   b. guided tours
   c. self-catering facilities
   d. four star accommodation

4 A function room of 70m² has
   a. a width of 10m and a height of 7m
   b. a width of 8m and a length of 9m
   c. a width of 10m and a length of 7m
   d. a width of 5m, a length of 4m and a height of 3½m

5 An overhead projector is used for showing
   a. films
   b. slides
   c. photographs
   d. transparencies

6 Translation

Translate the following words and expressions into your own language.

1 a. proportion, b. flight inclusive tour, c. fuel, d. promotional fares.

2 a. up-market, b. repeat visitors, c. activity holidays, d. escorted tours.

3 a. familiarization tour, b. leisure, c. optional visit, d. courier.

4 a. wide-bodied jets, b. American Plan, c. packed lunch, d. excursions.

5 a. joint destination, b. block booking, c. capacity, d. delegates.

6 a. interconnected, b. postpone, c. trade media, d. overhead projector.

7 Verbs and nouns

Complete the following table.

verb	noun	verb	noun
1 grow	......	9 expand	......
2 promote	......	10	budget
3	participant	11	negotiation
4 increase	......	12 postpone	......
5 arrange	......	13 propose	......
6	launch	14	liaison
7 demand	......	15	quotation
8 exhibit	......	16 recommend	......

8 Abbreviations

What do the following abbreviations stand for?

1 ft^2	4 ASAP	7 ATTN	10 PLS
2 TLX	5 OCC	8 FAM	11 AV
3 FIT	6 RE	9 EEE	12 HKD

9 Writing

Join each of the part sentences in the top group to one of the part sentences in the bottom group, using one of the connectors in the box.

1 The conference will not be held ...
2 Conference centres are usually chosen ...
3 The York tour was very successful ...
4 The group didn't miss the plane ...
5 Hotels should not accept conferences ...
6 The operators didn't arrange the package ...

because of
so
unless
although

a ... they were offered good rates.
b ... their good communications.
c ... the operator expanded the York programme.
d ... 400 or more people register as delegates.
e ... they were late arriving at the airport.
f ... they have the necessary space and equipment.

10 Description

Answer the following questions.

1 Explain the difference between
   a. an independent tour and an escorted tour
   b. American Plan and Continental Plan
   c. group rates and rack rates
   d. a manager and a proprietor
2 Describe four types of activity holiday.
3 What is the purpose of a familiarization tour?
4 List the kind of technical equipment that is needed at a conference.
5 What is the purpose of a release-back clause in a contract?

Complete the following flow diagram of a tour operator's FIT planning, using the information on the next page.

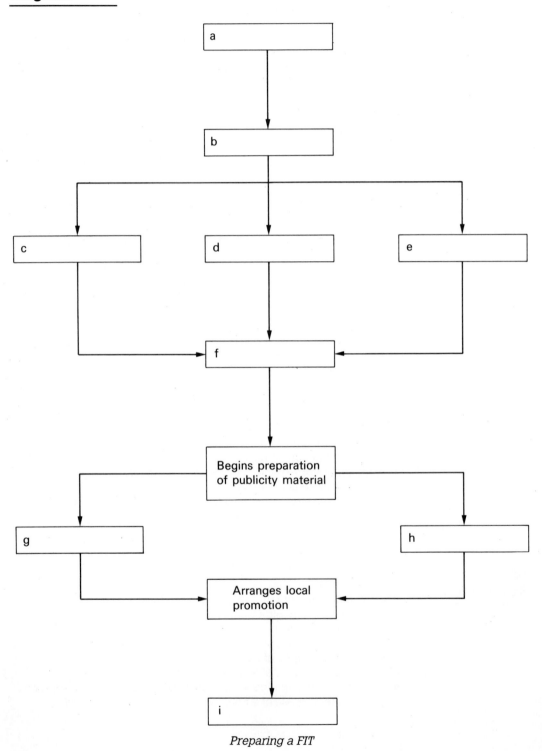

Preparing a FIT

1 Arranges for local journalists to visit area
2 Negotiates for excursions
3 Launches package
4 Negotiates rates with carrier
5 Makes FAM of area
6 Signs contracts with hotelier, handling agent, and tour company
7 Negotiates for transfers
8 Sends counter staff to visit area
9 Negotiates for accommodation

Key

In the following Key, the symbol △ has been used to show that this is a model answer; there are other possible answers.

Unit 1

Reading and Listening

Reading check

1 In a small hotel, the work of a receptionist may also include the job of advance reservations clerk, enquiry clerk, and book-keeper. 2 The advance reservations clerk. 3 Telephone; telex; telegram; letter; computer terminal; personal contact. 4 When they make bookings by telephone. 5 He/She records it on a reservation form and in a reservation diary.

Listening check

1 A double room with bath. 2 They are less expensive and quieter. 3 He must pay the maximum price. 4 It's medium-sized. 5 He needs a room for 17th and 18th August.

Language study

Requesting information

1 Could you tell me your telephone number, please? 2 Would you repeat your surname, please? 3 Could you tell me the number of people in the group, please? 4 Can you give me your arrival time, please? 5 Could you spell the street name, please? 6 Can you confirm your date of departure, please?

Comparing

3 The Station Hotel is more convenient than the Hotel Park. The Hotel Bristol is the most convenient. 4 The Hotel Bristol is less comfortable than the Hotel Park. The Station Hotel is the most comfortable. 5 The Station Hotel is bigger than the Hotel Park. The Hotel Bristol is the biggest of the three. 6 The Hotel Bristol is more modern than the Hotel Park. The Station Hotel is the least modern.

two thousand, seven hundred and fourteen; the thirtieth of April, nineteen eighty-three; oh eight five eight two three six two; twelve thousand, four hundred and forty-nine; June the twelfth; room three hundred and seventeen; oh one seven oh three double four six eight; the nineteenth of July; room five oh two; six hundred and fifty; the fifth floor; May the fourteenth nineteen eighty-two; oh one four double five four oh double one; the thirtieth of November nineteen eighty-two; the twelfth floor; the ninth of July nineteen eighty-four; seventeen thousand, four hundred and forty-six.

Listening and Speaking

Listening

1st caller: James; 21 August; Mr and Mrs; pm; 6 nights; 42 Station Road, York, YO2 1JG; 0904 53666; twin bath; 390 crowns; two people. 2nd caller: not necessary. 3rd caller: Lang; 24 August; Mr; one night; Holstein AG, Postweg 45, 2000 Hamburg 22; single; one person. (Note: bill to company.) 4th caller: Roberts; 19 August; Mr and Mrs; 4 nights; P.O. Box 743, NL-1017 Amsterdam; 02 16 45 72; double shower; 340 crowns per person; two people. (Note: full board; garage.)

Activities

A **1** Four **2** Yes **3** Six **4** Yes **5** 19 August

Writing

1 Dear Mr Giles, Thank you for your letter. We have pleasure in confirming your booking of a double room with shower from 3 April for three nights. Your room is on a lower floor. A deposit is not required. We look forward to your visit. Yours sincerely, ... **2** Dear Mr Gilbert, Thank you for your letter. We have pleasure in confirming your booking of a twin room with bath from 2 June for seven nights. We have reserved a quiet room for you as requested. A deposit is not required. We look forward to your visit. Yours sincerely, ... **3** Dear Mrs Gregory, Thank you for your letter. We have pleasure in confirming your booking of a single room from 6 June for four nights. We have also reserved a garage space for you for the same period. A deposit is not required. We look forward to your visit. Yours sincerely, ... △

Unit 2

Reading and Listening

Reading check

1 The guest's name, nationality, home address, and signature and, for foreign visitors, passport information.   2 To make sure that the information is correct and legible.   3 The receptionist should obtain the original hotel voucher.   4 It is not necessary for the receptionist to deal with each member of the group.   5 The room board, the Whitney Room Status Rack, and electronic room status.

Listening check

Key Card: John Rawson; Room 708; 24th; one guest; SB; 30,000 lire; 27th.

1 Because he'll need it as identification.   2 In the evening.   3 It never closes.   4 The porter will show him to his room.

Language study

Asking questions

1 Can you change your booking, Mr Jones?   2 Will you confirm in writing, madam?   3 Are you cancelling your reservation, Mr Laker?   4 Which tour group are you with, sir?   5 Where is your next destination, sir?   6 Has the tour group arrived?   7 Have you checked the registration card?   8 Who are you waiting for, Mrs Masters?   9 Why are you leaving earlier than expected, Mr Qatan?   10 Do you want an early call, sir?

Describing people's jobs

1 A person who/that deals with enquiries.   2 What is an advance reservations clerk?   3 A person who/that carries bags and shows guests to their rooms.   4 What is a travel agent?   5 A person who/that works in an office.   6 A person who/that deals with money.

Nations, nationalities and currency

1 French, Franc.   2 Spain, Peseta.   3 Britain, Pound.   4 Italian, Lire.   5 Greek, Drachma.   6 Danish, Danish Crown.   7 The Netherlands (Holland), Guilder.   8 Switzerland, Swiss Franc.   9 Germany, Marks.   10 Japanese, Yen.   11 United States, Dollar.   12 Mexican, Peso.   13 Sweden, Swedish Crown.   14 Austrian, Schilling.   15 Belgian, Franc.   16 Portugal, Escudo.

Advising

1 You should always prepare the arrival list.   **2** You should always remember your Hotel Voucher.   **3** You should always remember to confirm a booking.   **4** You should always be polite to the guests. **5** You should always note down the customer's name.

Listening and Speaking

Listening

1 T   **2** F   **3** T   **4** T   **5** T   **6** F   **7** T   **8** T

Activities

A   **1** Nationality   **2** Home Address   **3** Foreign   **4** Passport Number   **5** Place of Issue   **6** Next   **7** Signature   **8** 708 **9** 1   **10** 30,000 Lire   **11** 24th August

C   **1** The receptionist allocates a room.   **2** Room slot   **3** Alphabetical rack   **4** Telephonist   **5** Porter's desk   **6** The slip is removed and crossed through with a red pencil.   **7** Staff remove guest's slip.

Writing

1 Dear Mr Cook, Thank you for your letter. We have, as you requested, changed your booking from one twin with bath from 22 – 28 July to one twin with bath from 23 – 29 July. We note that you will be arriving at 17.00. Yours sincerely, ...   **2** Dear Mrs Pettersson, Thank you for your letter. We have, as you requested, changed your booking from two doubles for 8 nights from 14 August to two doubles for 6 nights from 14 August. Yours sincerely, ...   **3** Dear Mr Archer, Thank you for your letter. We are sorry to hear that you cannot now visit Brindisi. We have, as you requested, cancelled your booking. Yours sincerely, ...   △

Unit 3

Reading and Listening

Reading check

1 All meals except breakfast.   2 The guests do, using shoe cleaning machines.   3 The guest is.   4 The Housekeeper, Reception, or the Duty Manager.   5 In the rooms.

Listening check

1 He has bad pains in his chest.   2 His breathing is weak, but his temperature is normal.   3 She should loosen her husband's clothes and keep him warm.   4 When she pays the hotel bill.   5 He is going there to collect the prescription.

Language study

Reporting messages

1 'Mrs Betts said she had a message for you, Mr Graham.'   2 'Mr Tor said he needed some soap.'   3 'Mrs Reid said she'd see you in the lobby, Mr Reid.'   4 'Mr Parks said he was going to the shops, Mrs Parks.'   5 'The manager said we needed the registration cards.'
6 'Mr Jones said he wanted his bill.'   7 'Mr Lambert said he'd collected the newspaper, Mrs Lambert.'   8 'Your sister said that she was leaving at two, Mrs Pritchard.'

Using nouns in groups

1 facilities for making tea   2 leader of a tour group   3 room service   4 airline seat reservation system   5 machine for cleaning shoes   6 telephone area code   7 accommodation bureau
8 overseas guest registration form   9 list of arrivals   10 system for showing the status of rooms

Using the passive

2 Newspapers can be ordered at the desk.   3 Registration cards must be signed on arrival.   4 Reservations should be confirmed in writing.   5 Traveller's cheques can be changed at the cash desk.
6 Keys should be left at Reception.

Listening and Speaking

1 Room 200; 5.30 early call tomorrow.   **2** John Steel; room 370; Mr Pettersson.   **3** Room 342; send up hot milk and aspirins.   **4** Fairfax; help with changing flights needed.

Activities

A **b** 5,6 **c** 1 **d** .5 **e** 6,8 **f** 8 **g** 2 **h** 1,8 **i** 4 **j** 6,8 **k** 4,8 **l** 1,8 **m** 2,3 **n** 6,8 **o** 6,8 **p** 8 **q** 7

B **1** Two – BA 561 and OA 259 **2** Because it makes one stop.
3 Three – BA 561, OA 259 and KU 191 **4** All except OA 261 **5** Four – SQ, BA, OA and KU **6** One hour

Writing

1 Mr Brown is leaving at 3 pm this afternoon. He's catching a flight to London at Hellenikon Airport at 6 pm.   **2** Mrs Curtis has ordered a taxi for 10.30 am. She will meet her brother at the entrance to the Akropolis at 11.00 am.   **3** Miss Wiseman has cancelled her order for the 'Times' newspaper. She would like to order the 'International Herald Tribune' instead.   **4** Mr Drew, who made a booking for three nights in a single room with bath from 21 March 1982, has sent a letter confirming the booking.   **5** Mrs Payne called the doctor at 9 am because her husband was ill. The doctor sent Mr Payne to the City Hospital at 11 am.   **6** John Adams left a message for Mr Authur at midday that he would not be able to meet him in the Diplomat Bar at 7 pm this evening.

Unit 4

Reading and Listening

Reading check

1 It recommends restaurants with high quality cuisine. **2** A one star restaurant is good but a two star restaurant is very good. **3** The basic charge includes service and VAT. **4** No, only when you see the letters 'b.i.' **5** Three.

Listening check

1 He recommends the beef chasseur. **2** The hors d'oeuvres followed by the mackerel. **3** John. **4** It's served with spaghetti. **5** A half bottle of Chablis and a Beaujolais.

Language study

Making suggestions

2 If you feel hungry, sir, why don't you try the English breakfast? **3** If you're looking for a good restaurant, madam, what about trying the Good Eating Guide? **4** If you have a headache, sir, I'd suggest an aspirin. **5** If it's a long way to walk, madam, why don't you take a taxi? **6** If you feel very hot, sir, I'd suggest a beer. **7** If you've had a tiring day, madam, why don't you have a rest? △

Describing dishes and drinks

1 That's three parts gin mixed with one part dry Martini and served with an olive. **2** It's rice and sea food cooked together and served in the cooking dish. **3** It's veal cooked with carrots and onions and served in a white sauce with boiled rice. **4** It's coffee mixed with brown sugar, Irish whiskey, and cream and served as an after-dinner drink. **5** That's pieces of pork fried and served in a sugar and vinegar sauce with rice.

Present time

1 No, I haven't. I'm still waiting for the menu. **2** No, I haven't. I'm still looking for it. **3** Has the 'Times' arrived yet? **4** Have you telephoned your company yet? **5** Have you completed the registration form yet? **6** No, I haven't. I'm still using it. **7** Have you allocated the tour group yet? **8** No, I haven't. I'm still cleaning it.

Listening and Speaking

Dialogue 1 one fresh orange juice; one fresh grapefruit juice; bacon, egg and tomato; two soft-boiled eggs; toast, butter and marmalade; tea with lemon; 7.30 am; Mr and Mrs Sands; room 226. **Dialogue 2** a Campari with plenty of ice and soda; a cold bottle of lager; a Scotch on the rocks; a glass of well-chilled dry white wine; Mr Carter; room 714. **Dialogue 3** a ham sandwich; a pâté sandwich; a coffee (white); a shandy; Mrs Taylor; room 302.

Activities

A **1** acde **2** bcd **3** ac **4** acdf **5** acd **6** abdef **7** acdef
8 acd **9** abc **10** ac **11** abcdf **12** abc **13** abdf **14** bd **15** d
16 a **17** e **18** acde

B 6–2–9–8–3–10–11–5–4–1–7

Writing

A **1** As requested, we have booked you two double rooms which look over the park. **2** Here is our service list that gives details of the services available at the hotel. **3** You can buy cigarettes and sweets at the hotel tobacconist which is situated in the hotel lobby. **4** Mr Franks is one of the duty managers who deal with day to day problems. **5** There are free shoe cleaning machines available which can be found on the 2nd and 5th floors. **6** We have received a telephone booking from European Mines who will confirm by telex.
7 The porter has gone to the chemist for the prescription which he will bring to your room. **8** The Café Tour specializes in salmon dishes which are only served in season. **9** There is a car park adjoining the hotel where only hotel guests may leave their cars.
10 The hotel has a coffee shop on the ground floor where beverages and snacks are served all day.

B The Hotel Simon has two restaurants which are situated on the ground floor and first floor. The first-floor restaurant is called the Grill which has only an à la carte menu. The other restaurant is called the Simon where a set menu is usually served. Monsieur Noiret is the reception head waiter who deals with table reservations in the Grill and the Simon which are both very popular. The Grill is particularly busy in the evening and so it is always necessary to reserve a table well in advance. In fact, the Grill is an excellent restaurant where first-rate cuisine and good wines are always available.

Revision Unit 1

1 Asking questions

1 How long does Mr Wright want to stay? 2 When did Mrs Sloane check out? 3 Would they rather have white wine? 4 Which room are the Lepics staying in? 5 Was the manager responsible? 6 Who should the Browns write to? 7 How many non-stop London flights a day are there? 8 When is she leaving the hotel? 9 When does the Golden Ball restaurant close? 10 What would they like for dessert?

2 Vocabulary

1 receipt 2 external 3 currency 4 in 5 vacant 6 to 7 deposit 8 entrée

3 Comprehension

1 Sealink from Dover or Folkestone 2 Three – Sealink, Seaspeed, and Townsend Thoresen 3 £2 4 Yes, the cost is exactly the same. 5 North Sea Ferries from Hull, and Townsend Thoresen from Felixstowe 6 On Tor Line from Felixstowe

4 Verb tenses and forms

1 is growing 2 leaves 3 checked in 4 is still waiting 5 should be chilled 6 does not confirm 7 were confirmed 8 haven't looked at 9 rings 10 can be changed

5 Multiple choice

1 d 2 d 3 c 4 c 5 d 6 a 7 c

7 Verbs and nouns

2 reservation 3 booking 4 identify 5 enquiry 6 alteration 7 clarify 8 telex 9 cancel 10 selection 11 allocation 12 signature 13 cash 14 recommend 15 charge 16 registration

8 Letter writing

1 Dear Mr Freeman, Thank you for your letter. We have pleasure in confirming that we have booked a double room for you from 7 June 1982 for four nights. The room has a view over the park. A deposit is not required. We look forward to your visit. Yours sincerely, ...
2 Dear Mrs Dobson, Thank you for your letter. We have, as requested, reserved two adjoining singles for you for a period of a fortnight starting on 21 July 1982. A deposit is not required. We look forward to your visit. Yours sincerely, ... 3 Dear Miss Massoni, Thank you for your letter. We have, as requested, reserved a second single room for you for the night of 18.8.82. We have also reserved a garage space for you. We look forward to your visit. Yours sincerely, ... △

10 Job descriptions

1 Restaurant Manager 2 Head Waiter 3 Head Receptionist 4 Reception Waiter 5 Station Waiter 6 Advance Reservations Clerk 7 Enquiry Clerk 8 Receptionist 9 Cashier 10 Head Porter 11 Night Porter

Unit 5

Reading and Listening

1 Filleting, carving, and cooking speciality dishes at the table.
2 Because it is fast and requires less equipment. 3 Silver service and plate service. 4 The food is served on silver flats instead of on plates. 5 Because it is the cheapest form of service.

1 So that they can watch the people in the street. 2 It consists of three courses. 3 Because they don't know any Arabic or much French. 4 Soup and steak. 5 Well done for Mrs Drayton and rare for Mr Drayton. 6 Very dry red wine.

Language study

Preference

3 Do you prefer steak or chicken? I prefer steak but Mr Sobell prefers chicken. 4 Would you rather sit inside or outside? I'd rather sit outside but Mr Sobell would rather sit inside. 5 Would you rather pay by cash or by credit card? I'd rather pay by cash but Mr Sobell would rather pay by credit card. 6 Would you rather order now or later? I'd rather order now but Mr Sobell would rather order later.
7 Do you prefer the table d'hôte menu or à la carte? I prefer the à la carte menu, but Mr Sobell prefers the table d'hôte. 8 Do you prefer coffee at the table or in the lounge? I prefer coffee at the table but Mr Sobell prefers coffee in the lounge.

Degree

1 No, it's not dry enough. I like it very dry. 2 I'm afraid it's too spicy. I can't eat it. 3 I'm afraid you're too early. You will have to wait.
4 No, it's not early enough. I must leave very early. 5 I'm afraid it's too strong. I can't drink it. 6 I'm afraid it's too big. I can't stay there. 7 No, it's not weak enough. I like them very weak. 8 I'm afraid it's too warm. I like cooler rooms.

Word order

1 An à la carte menu is always available in the Dar Marhaba restaurant in the evening. 2 They never ate very well in the hotel restaurant. 3 The waiter often laid the table badly. 4 Sixty rooms are reserved by Johnson Tours in the Hotel Park in August. 5 The gueridon waiter always carved the roast beef skilfully. 6 The Night Porter was on duty at ten o'clock every evening.

Listening and Speaking

Listening

1 8.00 – 9.30 **2** 12.30 – 2.00 pm **3** 7.00 – 8.30 and 8.30 – 10.00 pm
4 Vegetarians (3) **5** Diabetic **6** Sandwiches and snacks, soft drinks and fruit.

Activities

A **1** e **2** i **3** t **4** l **5** b **6** c **7** o **8** q **9** j **10** a **11** p
12 k **13** u **14** h **15** n **16** r **17** d **18** g **19** s **20** f **21** m

B **1** Sherry, Vermouth, Campari **2** Champagne **3** Chablis, Hock, Riesling **4** Rosé d'Anjou **5** Beaujolais, Beaune, Burgundy, Chianti, Rioja **6** Port, Madeira **7** Liqueur Brandy, Cointreau **8** Hors d'oeuvres **9** Hors d'oeuvres **10** Fish, Chicken **11** Veal, Chicken **12** Beef, Lamb **13** Dessert **14** Coffee

Writing

1 Dear Mr and Mrs Sharp, Thank you for your letter of .... I am afraid that we do not have a double room with bath available for fourteen nights from 17 May. We have a double without bath for that period. If that is not convenient I can recommend the Hotel Belami which is in the same chain as us and of the same standard. They have a double with bath for the period you require. If you will let me know what you would like, I will make the necessary booking for you. Yours sincerely, ... **2** Dear Mr Grimes, Thank you for your letter of .... I am afraid it is not possible for us to reserve a room for you during the period you require. There is a large international convention in Sfax that week and, because of this, very little hotel accommodation is available. Yours sincerely, ... **3** Dear Mr Huppert, Thank you for your letter of .... It is possible for us to extend your booking as you require. Unfortunately there is no single with bath vacant during the three extra days, so it would be necessary for you to move to a single with shower. If that is not convenient I can recommend the Hotel Belami which is in the same chain as us and of the same standard. They have a single with bath for the full ten day period you require. If you will let me know what you would like, I will make the booking for you. Yours sincerely, ... △

Unit 6

Reading and Listening

Reading check

1 It is situated off the coast and to the north of Estartit.   **2** Swimming, fishing, and sunbathing.   **3** Good boutiques and small souvenir shops.   **4** Because it is market day.   **5** The Club El Catalan, the Galeon, and the St. Tropez Discotheque.

Listening check

1 They're going to Madrid.   **2** At their hotel.   **3** From the top of the Christopher Columbus column.   **4** In a quarter of an hour.   **5** On shelves.

Language study

Using prepositions

1 from   **2** in   **3** out of   **4** at   **5** from   **6** off   **7** away from   **8** off   **9** on   **10** onto

Future time

1 am going   **2** is preparing   **3** departs   **4** are spending   **5** begins   **6** is meeting

Abbreviations

1 kilograms   **2** air conditioning   **3** Post Office   **4** pounds   **5** telephone   **6** kilometre   **7** departure   **8** degrees Centigrade   **9** number   **10** ounces   **11** stamped addressed envelope   **12** before midday   **13** hot and cold   **14** degrees Fahrenheit   **15** Street   **16** inclusive   **17** after midday   **18** hours   **19** Avenue   **20** Road   **21** francs   **22** arrival   **23** volts   **24** for example

Listening and Speaking

Listening

1 g   **2** h   **3** c   **4** b   **5** i   **6** d   **7** j   **8** f   **9** a   **10** e

Activities

B Mr Shaw 3. Mrs Ryan 1. Miss Berg 2.

Writing

1 Turn right outside the Post Office and walk down Alma Way until you come to Central Square. Cross the square and walk up Valley Road until you come to Tor Hill on the left. Go up Tor Hill and then take the first left into County Road. The zoo is a little way down on the left hand side. **2** Turn right outside the Cathedral, walk along Upham Road, and then take the first right into Circle Road. Continue as far as you can along Circle Road and then cross Union Street into County Road. The National Museum is a little way down on the right hand side. **3** Turn left outside the hotel and walk down Tor Hill. Turn right into Valley Road and then take the first left into Hudson Road. Walk to the end of Hudson Road, take the first left and then the first right and you will be in Old Town Road. The Central Bank is on the left hand side just past Bath Road. **4** Turn left outside the museum and walk along Parliament Street until it meets Park Road. Turn left into Park Road and continue walking along it and then Hudson Road until you come to Valley Road. Turn right and then take the first on your left. This is Tor Hill. The hotel is a little way up it on the right. **5** Turn left outside the hotel and walk down Tor Hill. Cross Valley Road and continue along Leopold Street until you get to Union Street. Turn right and continue until you can see Upham Road on your left. Cross the road and walk down Upham road. The Cathedral is on the left hand side. △

Unit 7

Reading and Listening

1 It was slow and the food was poor. 2 Because the hotel was not in the city centre. 3 It was left off the coach. 4 Some of them were rude when complaints were made. 5 Because of the bad service that was provided.

1 There is no water in the shower and no soap, towel, or toilet paper. 2 The most important thing is to fix it as soon as possible. 3 Because his plane was four hours late. 4 Because it was mentioned in the letter of confirmation. 5 She offers to book a room in a nearby hotel and arrange the transfer.

Language study

Causes of complaint

1 They should have made the bed. 2 They should have vacuumed the carpet. 3 They should have cleaned the ashtray. 4 They should have emptied the waste-paper basket. 5 They should have opened the curtains. 6 They should have removed the tray. 7 They should have picked up the books. 8 They should have replaced the lamp.

Getting things done

1 I'll have it fixed. 2 I'll have some sent up. 3 I'll have it repaired. 4 I'll have it delivered to your room. 5 I'll have it checked. 6 I'll have it brought down.

Adverbs of degree

1 Mr Lyons thought the souvenirs were extremely expensive. 2 It was quite hot on the beach yesterday afternoon. 3 Miss Rikard was very late for the meeting with the tour company. 4 He was very tired after the nine-hour flight from London. 5 Customers often complained about the rather high telephone charges. 6 Mrs Dill was extremely annoyed about the traffic noises from the street. △

Listening and Speaking

1 unfriendly; two rings and a gold watch stolen.   **2** Mr Smith, room 704; friendly; he was cut off twice while phoning his wife; contact the telephone company.   **3** Mr Jones; unfriendly; he thinks the wine is corked; (a) the steak will be changed (b) no action.

Activities

A   **1** Listen carefully   **2** Don't comment   **3** Make a short, clear apology   **4** Repeat the complaint   **5** Note down what the customer has said   **6** Deal with the complaint   **7** Inform the manager

Writing

1 Dear Mr Wainwright, The Hotel International is always interested to hear the comments of its guests and we are glad that you have written to us. I am extremely sorry that your meal in the Grill Restaurant was not up to our usual standard. I apologize for this and will make enquiries about it. We were extremely busy on the night you speak of and many of our staff were ill. I hope that we will continue to receive your custom and that, if you have a complaint, you will inform my staff immediately so that we can deal with the problem there and then. Yours sincerely, ...   **2** Dear Mrs Sherwood, Thank you for your letter of .... I am very sorry to hear that you have not yet received our brochure and price list. I apologize for this and am sending what you require together with this letter. Yours sincerely, ...   **3** Dear Mr Ambler, The Hotel International is always interested to hear the comments of its guests and we are glad that you have written to us. I am very sorry that you did not find the services provided by our hotel satisfactory. Most of our rooms are bigger than the room you were in but they are also more expensive. Our bar and restaurant prices are, we believe, normal for a hotel of this standard. I regret that the people in the next room were noisy. I hope we will continue to receive your custom and that, if you have a complaint, you will inform my staff immediately so that we can deal with the problem there and then. Yours sincerely, ...   △

Unit 8

Reading and Listening

Reading check

1 Machine billing has replaced the 'tab' in many smaller hotels. **2** It does foreign exchange calculations and holds credit card and ledger account details. **3** When the guest is ready to check out. **4** The control checks make the computer query charges that are not correctly posted. **5** Because the computer memory can hold credit card information.

Listening check

1 At the bottom **2** Meals and drinks **3** Five days **4** STD
5 Three

Language study

Past time

1 has been **2** left **3** checked in **4** has not visited **5** spent
6 came **7** has not paid **8** was **9** has liked **10** did not arrive

Quantity

1 information **2** British currency **3** minutes **4** beer **5** facilities
6 trouble **7** details **8** complaints

Calculating

1 one hundred and twenty plus forty-six minus ninety-two equals seventy-four **2** fourteen point one three five **3** seven eighths plus three quarters equals one and five eighths **4** four and a half times two equals nine **5** sixteen thousand, seven hundred and twenty
6 nine point three divided by three point one equals three **7** two and a quarter per cent **8** nine times three is twenty-seven **9** ten point five per cent **10** eighteen point seven one five

Listening and Speaking

Listening

1 meal; 460 pesos; credit card. **2** Mr Johnson; 1240 pesos; cash.
3 Mrs Bloom; coach tour; 6000 pesos.

Activities

A Ms Lamondou – 600 pesos. Mr Duensing – 436 pesos. Mr Ayyad – 1563.75 pesos. Mr and Mrs Ruiz – 1320 pesos.

B 301 – 3640 pesos. 302 – 3295 pesos. 303 – 6255 pesos. 304 – 5315 pesos. 305 – 3140 pesos.

Writing

1 You can buy whisky in town, but it's cheaper at the airport. OR You can buy whisky in town. However, it's cheaper at the airport. **2** They didn't have any cash on them. Therefore they had to use their credit cards. OR They didn't have any cash on them, so they had to use their credit cards. **3** The sightseeing trip goes through the old quarter as well as the modern city centre. **4** There is a radio and a colour TV in the room. OR There is a radio in the room, as well as a colour TV.

When Mr Landseer arrived at the airport he wanted to hire a car, but the cost was rather high. He did not have enough cash on him, so he decided to use his credit card. Unfortunately when he felt in his pocket he found that his wallet was missing. His cheque book was missing, too. However, he did have his agent's telephone number, so he was able to ring for help.

Revision Unit 2

1 Prepositions

1 from, at **2** at, after **3** on, with, over **4** from, in, to, at **5** on, off **6** on, on **7** at, in **8** with

2 Vocabulary

1 tasks **2** events **3** souvenirs **4** comes to **5** meter **6** starters **7** stands for **8** self-service

3 Flow chart

1 j **2** m **3** a **4** e **5** c **6** f **7** n **8** g **9** h **10** k **11** d **12** b **13** i **14** l

4 Verb tenses and forms

1 left **2** should have arrived **3** is opening **4** will calculate **5** has been **6** were transferred **7** have not used **8** departs **9** will be provided **10** was not refunded

5 Multiple choice

1 c 2 a 3 c 4 b 5 d 6 c

7 Verbs and nouns

1 refund 2 calculate 3 entertainment 4 itemize 5 guide
6 economize 7 diet 8 statement 9 development 10 transfer
11 finance 12 apology 13 inhabitant 14 advertisement
15 comment 16 reduction

8 Letter writing

1 Dear Mr and Mrs Sykes, Thank you for your letter requesting a twin-bedded room with bath for seven nights from 16 September. Unfortunately we have no twin rooms vacant on the 16th. We could offer you six, or seven, nights from the 17th. Alternatively, the Bristol Hotel is close to us and is of similar standard and price. They have accommodation available for the days you requested. I look forward to hearing from you. Yours sincerely, ... 2 Dear Mr Rogers, Thank you for your letter enquiring about the Atlantic Room. Unfortunately it is not available on the day you require it. It was reserved some time ago. The Terrace Suite is not booked on 17 October, however, and we would be prepared to offer it to you at the same rate as the Atlantic Room. It is a little larger than the Atlantic Room and I am sure you would find it entirely suitable. I look forward to hearing from you soon. Yours sincerely, ... 3 Dear Miss Straw, The Hotel International is always interested to hear the comments of its guests and we are glad that you have written to us. I am extremely sorry that you did not find the services provided by our hotel satisfactory. We were short of staff during the period you were with us and our new computer billing system was giving us some trouble. These problems have now been solved. I hope we will continue to receive your custom and that, if you have a complaint, you will inform my staff immediately so that we can deal with the problem there and then. Yours sincerely, ... △

10 Calculations

The correct sterling totals are: 1 35.00 2 36.97 3 99.05 4 136.55
5 31.80 6 184.33 7 325.76 8 179.78 9 87.26 10 95.60

Unit 9

Reading and Listening

Reading check

1 By 4.7%   **2** Standbys and walk-on   **3** The number of people using cars and making repeat visits, the availability of promotional fares, and the cost of group accommodation   **4** Tour operators and travel agents who are capable of organizing FITs   **5** Travel trade journalists and travel agency staff

Listening check

1 Assistant Commercial Manager with the Yorkshire and Humberside Tourist Board   **2** In Utrecht   **3** In London   **4** Business visits
5 Types of accommodation to suit every preference and budget

Language study

Cause and effect

2 In 1976, the occupancy level was so high that group rates were not attractive.   **3** In 1977, there was such a heavy demand for tours that overbooking became a problem.   **4** In 1978, the summer was so hot that fewer people went abroad.   **5** In 1979, there was such a sudden reduction in fares that independent travel was more popular.
6 In 1981, a BBC series was so popular that more people went to Yorkshire. △

Using statistics

1 From 1975 to 1976, there was a 14% rise in the proportion of overseas visitors.   **2** Between 1974 and 1977, the proportion of overseas visitors expanded by 27%.   **3** The proportion of overseas visitors increased from 52% to 70% between 1975 and 1977.
4 Between 1975 and 1977, there was an 18% growth in the proportion of overseas visitors.   **5** There has been a 4% fall in the proportion of overseas visitors since last year.   **6** There was a decrease from 70% to 65% in the proportion of overseas visitors between 1977 and 1978.

Considering future possibilities

1 If fuel prices were reduced, the number of motoring holidays would rise.   **2** British holidays would become more popular, if the value of the pound was lower.   **3** If tourists complained more, standards of service would improve.   **4** Domestic resorts would benefit, if fewer people in the UK went on package tours abroad.   **5** Tourism would not expand rapidly, if the economic situation did not improve.   **6** If areas were not advertised, the level of tourist activity would not grow significantly.

Listening and Speaking

1 Tuesday at 3 **2** The possibility of fortnightly flights into Leeds/ Bradford from Copenhagen **3** General Manager **4** Monday at 10 **5** White Rose Hotel **6** Arrangements for a visit to the White Rose Hotel by tour operators.

Activities

A **1** From an Inter-City station or a British Rail Appointed Travel Agent **2** Families, senior citizens, and students **3** Accommodation, rail travel, reserved seats (most trains), station-hotel transfer, and travel across London (where appropriate) **4** Awayday, Weekend, Monthly, and Ordinary Returns **5** Britrail Travel International Inc, 222 Marylebone Road, London NW1 6JJ **6** One month

B **1** 2% **2** 7% **3** 5% **4** 15% **5** 7% **6** Japan **7** Benelux **8** France **9** Eire **10** USA **11** Canada **12** Australia **13** 11% **14** 6% **15** 7% **16** 4%

Writing

A **1** 200 Dutch and 200 German copies of the new Yorkshire brochure **2** YHTB **3** 12.57 **4** 15.05.82 **5** 27143 EFL G

B **1** PLS SEND 5 COPIES WHERE TO STAY IN YORKSHIRE TO DELFT TOUR HEAD OFFICE. THANK YOU IN ADVANCE – ATTN MARIA BAAN, RE WHERE TO STAY IN YORKSHIRE, NOT AVAILABLE UNTIL NEXT WEEK. WILL SEND 5 COPIES WHEN AVAILABLE AND ADVISE BY TLX. REGARDS ... **2** ATTN TONY JOHNSON, RE GERMAN JOURNALIST PARTY, PARTY NOT EXPECTED NOW UNTIL 6.30 ON 24.6.82. PLS CONFIRM YOU CAN MEET THEM THEN. REGARDS ... – ATTN JOHN GOULD, RE GERMAN JOURNALIST PARTY, OK. WILL MEET PARTY AT 6.30 ON 24.6.82. REGARDS ... **3** PLS SEND INFORMATION ON THE AVAILABILITY OF TOUR GUIDES FOR HALF AND FULL DAY SIGHTSEEING IN YORK PLUS RATES. REGARDS ... – ATTN PAUL BELMONDE, RE TOUR GUIDES IN YORK, GUIDES ARE AVAILABLE FROM 1 MAY TO 31 OCTOBER AT £30 PER FULL OR £20 PER HALF DAY. MAX NUMBER IN GROUP IS 15. REGARDS ... △

Unit 10

Reading and Listening

1 At the Berlin trade fair   2 Agreement with UK Airways on the travel arrangements   3 UK Airways   4 15 Texas tour operators and travel agents   5 To show the sightseeing attractions and the wide range of holiday types available in the region   6 It would like Mr Burwin to inform it if he is interested in joining the tour and if the dates are convenient.

1 Travel International   2 Traditional holidays   3 Singles, twins, doubles, and suites   4 No, the same   5 Four

Language study

1 There should be a good price from the carrier.   2 It was very windy over Europe so the plane might be late.   3 Your letter should arrive tomorrow.   4 Vista Voyages might be sending a representative.   5 There will be a number of problems with the schedule.   6 We might visit the Berlin trade fair.   7 UK 790 should arrive in twenty minutes.   8 There will be no train service on 25 December.

1 They left on 24 April.   2 Mr and Mrs Lopez have been occupying room 102 since 20 April.   3 He has been staying in York for business reasons.   4 They came for a holiday.   5 Mr and Mrs Chester have been staying the longest.   6 He has been having a holiday.

1 Does the White Rose have more twins than doubles?   2 Is the Roebuck bigger than the Carlton?   3 Is the discount in the White Rose the same as in the Roebuck?   4 Which hotel has the highest rack rate?   5 Do all the hotels have more twins than doubles?   6 Is the Carlton's full board rate less expensive than the White Rose's? 7 Which is the smallest hotel?   8 Is the discount in the Carlton as high as in the Roebuck?   9 Does the Carlton have fewer rooms than the other two hotels?   10 Which is the least expensive of the three hotels?   △

Listening and Speaking

1 Mr Sharp   **2** Car hire   **3** Cars for small tour groups two days a week in the summer   **4** Coach company   **5** A coach for a full day tour once a week during the summer   **6** Mr Mason   **7** Ross Travel   **8** Handling agent   **9** Transfers between the airport and the Crown Hotel for two tour groups a week May through September

Activities

A Day 1 –**1** 20.00   **2** Afternoon   **3** 19.30   **4** 07.20   **5** 10.30
Day 2 –**1**   10.00   **2** 19.00   **3** 12.30   **4** 22.30   **5** 17.30   **6** 08.30
7 09.30   **8** Afternoon   **9** 20.00
Day 3 –**1** 13.00   **2** 11.00   **3** 09.00   **4** 10.00   **5** 14.00

B   **1** e   **2** b   **3** j   **4** k   **5** a   **6** l   **7** d   **8** m   **9** c   **10** f   **11** h
12 g   **13** i

Writing

1 Most of the tour operators felt the FAM was valuable because it gave them a good idea of the region's tourist potential.   **2** The handling agent will deal with the transfers unless you prefer to make the arrangements yourself.   **3** Gunnar Andersson of Swedtour didn't join the group although he said he was coming.   **4** The idea of using the Crown Hotel was rejected because its manager couldn't accept the operator's offer.   **5** Companies providing local facilities don't usually offer discounts unless the operator can guarantee quite a large volume of business.   **6** Complimentary rooms are normally offered to couriers although there is usually a minimum group size needed for this.   **7** A surcharge will be necessary from 1 July unless the value of the pound falls.   **8** The tour operator made a detailed inspection of the hotel because he had to select suitable accommodation for a FIT.

Unit 11

Reading and Listening

Reading check

1 Because he had received a favourable offer from UK Airways.
2 He recommends Yorkshire as part of a joint-destination product.
3 Handling agents   4 Five   5 Because the brochure must soon be finalized.

Listening check

1 Two nights   2 A traditional Yorkshire dinner   3 Four courses, drinks before and during the meal, after-dinner coffee, and service.
4 Because the main course is roast beef.   5 A three-piece band.

Language study

Past time

1 After I had made an inspection of the hotel facilities, I made a report to the Managing Director.   2 After the group had attended a reception at the Globe Hotel, they had a guided tour of the city.   3 Before the tour operator agreed the '83 rates with the Falcon Hotel, he had visited five hotels in the region.   4 After the journalists had arrived at Hull, they travelled directly to Harrogate by coach.   5 Before Texas Travel included the Grand Hotel in their '83 bed plan, their representative had inspected the hotel.

Future time

4 I am reporting to the Managing Director at 9 am Tuesday next.
5 I am going to propose changes to the '83 program, at the next management meeting preferably.   6 I'll go on a FAM of Morocco in June or July perhaps.   7 I'm visiting an advertising agency on 2 June.   8 I'll write the UK report tomorrow, if there is time.   9 I'm going to sign the contract with Arrow Hotels as soon as possible.
10 I'm taking a day off next Friday.

Reporting questions

1 He wanted to know if the trade fair would be in February or March.   2 He asked why the carrier hadn't confirmed the flight costings.   3 She wanted to know when the New York flight was due.   4 He wondered whether the handling agent could arrange the tour.   5 They inquired how long Mr Pinar had been staying.   6 She asked me if that rate included all taxes.   7 He wanted to know where the meeting would take place.   8 He inquired if there was a supplement payable on single rooms.

Listening and Speaking

1 April through October **2** Four days **3** Friday through Tuesday
4 45 **5** 90 **6** None **7** Three months

Activities

A Tour Operator A: 1000 nights at £29 per night less 20% discount equals £2900 − £580 = £2320. Tour Operator B: 1000 nights × £23.50 = £2350. Tour Operator A has the better deal.

B **1** Dep Paris Nord 21.20 (Night Ferry). Arr London Victoria 07.45. Dep London King's Cross 09.00. Arr York 11.16. **2** Dep Paris Nord 08.10. Arr London Victoria 15.48. Dep London King's Cross 17.00. Arr York 19.11. Reservation London – York advisable. **3** Dep Paris Nord 21.20. Arr London Victoria 07.28. Dep London King's Cross 09.00. Arr York 11.16. **4** Dep Paris Nord 12.47 (reservation necessary). Arr London Charing Cross 18.40. Dep London King's Cross 07.32 (reservation advisable). Arr York 09.52.

Writing

1 Dear Mr Rossiter, re Full-day Tour Program for '83. I would like to confirm in writing the arrangements that we agreed last week for the 1983 program. 1 You will provide a full-day tour of the Yorkshire Dales (including stops at Reeth, Hawes, and Grassington) every Thursday from 6 May through 11 September inclusive. 2 You will pick up the group in a 35-seater bus at 09.15 at the Lawton Hotel, York. Set down will be at approximately 16.30 at the Lawton Hotel. I hope this represents the discussions we had. I would be grateful if you would let me know if you have any further comments. Meanwhile, I will have a contract drawn up. Yours sincerely, Leonard Bellman.
2 Dear Mr Stevens, re Hotel Arrangements for 1983. I would like to confirm in writing the arrangements we agreed last week for the 1983 season. 1 Schedule. From 2 May through 17 September, 56 people for three nights (Monday, Tuesday, Wednesday) weekly. Arrival 17.00 Monday, departure 09.00 Thursday. 2 Accommodation. You will provide 20 twin rooms with showers and 16 singles with showers. Full American Plan. We have an option on a further 20 twins in the period 30 July through 17 September. I hope this represents the discussions we had. I would be grateful if you would let me know if you have any further comments. Meanwhile, I will have a contract drawn up. Yours sincerely, Drew Masters.

3 Dear Mr Denton, I would like to confirm in writing the '83 transfer arrangements we agreed last week. 1 Every Tuesday from 1 May to 16 September you will pick up 59 passengers at Manchester Airport off UK 672 Houston – Manchester, arriving 11.25, for transfer to Grand Hotel, York. 2 Every Thursday from 10 May to 25 September you will pick up 59 passengers at Grand Hotel, York, for transfer to Manchester Airport for UK 312 Manchester – Paris CDG, departing 09.50. I hope this represents the discussions we had. I would be grateful if you would let me know if you have any further comments. Meanwhile, I will have a contract drawn up. Yours sincerely, Wilma Stanton. △

Unit 12

Reading and Listening

Reading check

1 Arranging for a 'Welcome' banner to be displayed at the airport and for Hong Kong public figures to provide welcome addresses at opening ceremonies and dinner functions. **2** By giving advice on Customs and Immigration procedures. **3** By providing supplies of promotional literature for mailing to potential delegates. **4** In the Association's calendar 'Coming Meetings, Conferences, and Exhibitions'. **5** Accompanying persons.

Listening check

1 About 160 **2** Over 2000 square feet **3** 200 **4** Telex, photocopying, and secretarial services **5** Movie, slide, and overhead projectors.

Language study

Future time

1 International Hotels Inc will have built their new conference centre by the end of the year. **2** The committee will very soon have finalized the preparations for the group. **3** The housekeeping staff will have cleaned those rooms in an hour. **4** All the delegates will have received this information at least a month before the conference.
5 The delegates will all have arrived within two or three hours. **6** UK Airways will not have introduced new aircraft on this route before the late eighties.

Dimensions

What is the height of the first room? The height is 10 feet. What is the area of the second room? The area is 260 square metres. How long is the second room? It's 26 metres long. What is the width of the first room? The width is 12 feet. △

Gerund and Infinitive

1 holding   **2** to send   **3** to contact   **4** organizing   **5** to bring   **6** to confirm   **7** preparing/to prepare   **8** making

Listening and Speaking

Listening

Conference Enquiry Form: **1** Int'l conf   **3** International Association of Shopping Centre Managers, 35 Curzon Street, London W1Y 2AC   **4** 14 November 5 days   **5** Delegates 240 International Delegates 210 Hong Kong Delegates 30   **6** 90 twins and 30 singles   **7** 240 persons
Set up: theatre, 5 meeting rooms.
Conference Package Breakdown of Costs:
a 1368   **b** 30   **c** welcome reception   **d** 240   **e** farewell banquet
f island tour   **g** 1900

Activities

A   Preliminary Announcement: 3 7 11 12 14
Second Announcement: 1 2 4 5 6 8 9 10 13

B   **1** c   **2** b   **3** g   **4** a   **5** f   **6** d   **7** h   **8** e

Writing

1 ATTN PAUL HENNELL, RE HONG KONG VISIT, I CONFIRM 6 SINGLES BOOKED FOR 3 NIGHTS. PLS SEND ASAP COMMITTEE ARRIVAL DETAILS. REGARDS – ATTN YUNG LAM, RE HONG KONG VISIT, ONLY 5 REPEAT 5 NOW COMING. PLS CANCEL 1 SINGLE. ARRIVING BA 3 15.15 THURSDAY 13 AUGUST. REGARDS
2 ATTN JOOS PLESMAN, RE IASCM HONG KONG CONFERENCE, MAY I REMIND YOU THAT THERE IS A LATE REGISTRATION FEE. WE HAVE NOT RECEIVED ANY REGISTRATIONS FROM YOU. REGARDS – ATTN PAUL HENNELL, RE IASCM HONG KONG CONFERENCE, SORRY ABOUT THE DELAY. PLS REGISTER 3 DELEGATES AND 2 ACCOMPANYING PERSONS FOR US. DETAILS FOLLOW. REGARDS

3 ATTN RESERVATION MANAGER, IASCM CONFERENCE, I CONFIRM THAT WE REQUIRE THE 160 TWINS AND 45 SINGLES PREVIOUSLY BOOKED. WE ALSO NEED AN ADDITIONAL 20 TWINS. CAN YOU HELP US? REGARDS – ATTN PAUL HENNELL, RE IASCM CONFERENCE, WE CAN OFFER ONLY 5 ADDITIONAL TWINS. WE HAVE 15 DOUBLES HOWEVER. WILL THEY BE OK? PLS CONFIRM ASAP. REGARDS △

Revision Unit 3

1 Verbs and prepositions

1 on **2** in **3** in **4** with **5** by **6** with **7** with **8** on

2 Vocabulary

1 surcharge **2** occupancy **3** optional **4** sponsored **5** contract **6** venue **7** preliminary **8** valid

3 Comprehension

1 No, infants (ages 0–2) do not have this allowance. **2** International Route Charges **3** £276 **4** Airport tax on departure from the Caribbean **5** 10½ hours **6** £311 **7** Meals and wine **8** £1207.50

4 Verb tenses and forms

1 was opened **2** come **3** was **4** will not have finished **5** has been staying **6** leaves **7** had arrived **8** has **9** using **10** have not been held

5 Multiple choice

1 b **2** a **3** c **4** c **5** d

7 Verbs and nouns

1 growth **2** promotion **3** participate **4** increase **5** arrangement **6** launch **7** demand **8** exhibition **9** expansion **10** budget **11** negotiate **12** postponement **13** proposal **14** liaise **15** quote **16** recommendation

8 Abbreviations

1 square feet **2** telex **3** flight inclusive tour **4** as soon as possible **5** subscriber is engaged **6** concerning **7** attention **8** familiarization tour **9** error **10** please **11** audio-visual **12** Hong Kong dollar(s)

9 Writing

1 The conference will not be held unless 400 or more people register as delegates. **2** Conference centres are usually chosen because of their good communications. **3** The York tour was very successful, so the operator expanded the York programme. **4** The group didn't miss the plane, although they were late arriving at the airport. **5** Hotels should not accept conferences unless they have the necessary space and equipment. **6** The operators didn't arrange the package, although they were offered good rates.

11 Flow Diagram

1 g **2** d **3** i **4** a **5** b **6** f **7** e **8** h **9** c

Word list

Appendix 1
Useful vocabulary

Room types

---

single	15
twin	15
double	15
adjoining rooms	26
suite	69
function rooms	148
interconnected rooms	148
hospitality room	152

Holiday, tour, and travel types

---

independent travel	112
familiarization trips	112
flight inclusive tours	112
traditional holidays	125
activity holidays	124
escorted tours	124
hotel packages	124
special seasonal tours	124
family-oriented packages	124
self-catering arrangements	124
independent tours	124
joint-destination tours	134

Hotel accommodation arrangements

European Plan	143	bed only
Continental Plan	137	bed and breakfast
modified American Plan	137	bed, breakfast and lunch or dinner
half board	—	
demi-pension	—	
full board	9	bed, breakfast, lunch and dinner
American Plan	137	

Appendix 2
British English and American English

British English		American English
aircraft	40	airplane
bill	16	check
book-keeper	9	bookkeeper
car hire	34	car rental
chips	62	French Fries
city centre	84	downtown
coach	84	bus
engaged	120	busy
fill in	24	fill out
first floor	—	second floor
ground floor	—	first floor
grill	51	broil
hall porter	34	bell captain
lift	24	elevator
May to September	128	May through September
notes	110	bills
pavement	74	sidewalk
porter	24	bellboy, bellman, bell hop
programme	143	program
pubs	132	saloons
put through (telephone call)	15	connect
railway station	12	train station
receptionist	9	room clerk
return (ticket)	159	two way, round trip (ticket)
single (ticket)	—	one way (ticket)
taps	93	faucets
tin	49	can
traveller's cheques	34	travelers checks
trunk call	96	long distance call
underdone	62	rare
wardrobe	86	closet
wash basin	93	washbowl
waste-paper basket	86	wastebasket